GRAND DISHES

Anastasia Miari & Iska Lupton

GRAND DISHES

Recipes and stories from
grandmothers of the world

unbound

First published in 2021

Unbound
Level 1, Devonshire House
One Mayfair Place
London W1J 8AJ
www.unbound.com

Text design by Studio Behn

Images © Ella Louise Sullivan
Mercedes, Gloria, Zena, Shewa, Ciccina, Rajni, Jean, Anastasia,
Vera, Flora, Fina, Dagmar, Clara Maria, Tigger, Tinh, Margit,
June, Nicole, Nicoletta and Mualla

Images © Iska Lupton
Harriet, Helen, Dora, Tish, Chula, Sharon, Maral, Tootsie, Irma,
Dolores, Westelle, Darcelle and Anne

Images © Nina Raasch   Images © Anastasia Miari
Edna, Ester and Ania   Juana Maria

Images © Maureen Evans   Images © Issy Croker
Betsy   Jenny

A CIP record for this book is available from the British Library

ISBN 978-1-80018-000-0 (hardback)
ISBN 978-1-80018-001-7 (ebook)

Printed in Slovenia by DZS

3 5 7 9 8 6 4 2

This book is not about what it's like to be old.
It's about what it's like to have lived.

CONTENTS

FOREWORD

There were lots of meals that I could have asked Granny to make for our arrival at her house in Norfolk. But I always asked for kedgeree: all buttery onions and milky rice and smoky haddock and plenty of hard-boiled eggs from toothless-Fred-down-the-road's hens. In that oft-cited Proustian way, each time I had it, I'd not only appreciate that portion, but reappreciate portions past.

I find it poignant now that kedgeree was the thing I honed in on from Granny's repertoire because it had been significant in her own childhood, too. She spent her early years in Jaipur, India, when Britain was just a concept to her, an idea perpetuated by cooked breakfasts, tea and cake – and kedgeree. Her kedgeree, and many other things she cooked, seasoned my childhood with salt, fat and love, and made food into so much more than fuel: it took on an imaginative quality. Dishes and tastes and the smell of things cooking became associated with people and stories, places and moments.

I don't have an accurate recipe for Granny's kedgeree. She never followed one. All quantities were approximate and generous. The recipe died with her; I think only she could make it that good. I just wish I'd had the initiative to do what Anastasia Miari and Iska Lupton have done, and recorded Granny making it, chatting while she did so, hearing the memories she associated with kedgeree and learning how to make it as she did, so I could now make it for my daughter. A recipe not only accompanies us through life, it can outlive us if we arm the next generation with the wherewithal to make it; an edible baton.

Grand Dishes captures that passing-on to preserve both the recipes and the characters who make them. In these pages, you'll find some 70 grandmother recipes, accompanied by stories, sageness (for both cooking and life) and snapshots. The motto of this book – 'It's not about what it's like to be old, it's about what it's like to have lived' – recognises the dignity and wisdom inherent to old age.

So how important it is to record their voices, then, before they are lost entirely. Theirs is perhaps the last generation of women not to have had a public life, who are (mostly) strangers to the technologies so inextricable from the modern day; their worlds were largely domestic, smaller than mine is, but perhaps all the richer for that simplicity. *Grand Dishes* is as much a celebration of the unselfconsciousness of its subjects going about their business irrespective of trends and external pressures as it is of their food.

I've been thinking a lot about the things I want my daughter to associate with my cooking. At age one, she's just starting to recognise flavours and, with kedgeree and the rest of my own culinary inheritance in mind, I'm excited to lay the foundations of what home tastes like for her and, maybe one day, my grandchildren.

—

Mina Holland

ORIGINS

My Greek Yiayia Anastasia (who you'll find on page 111) is the inspiration behind *Grand Dishes*. Before Iska and I ambitiously set out to document the recipes of the world's grandmothers, this began as a personal project to finally pin down Yiayia's recipes.

One of the eldest of ten siblings who was put to work 'out on the land' and never went to school, Yiayia had an education in planting by the moon's cycle, wild-herb foraging, sourdough-bread baking and cooking rich Corfiot dishes like cinnamon *stifado* stew in a pot over a fire she would build herself.

Stoic, cutting and at times just plain terrifying, Yiayia is not the kind of granny you go to for cuddles. She has a look of disapproval that could kill. She once famously tied my dad - then just seven years old - to a tree with an ant's nest at his feet as a punishment. In the kitchen though, she is all heart.

For Yiayia, food is love. Feeding our family is how she shows us she loves us. Our meals together as a family are characterised with shouty disputes and wild cackles of laughter (often from her). The food is simple, made up of Yiayia's own produce and never anything less than delicious.

From Yiayia, I have inherited this need to feed, to make mealtimes a social occasion for mutual connection. This project started with my wanting to share the special recipes that take me back to a place where I have felt most loved, at my grandmother's dining table.
—

Anastasia Miari

My German grandmother 'Lally' (Margit on page 185) inspired us to capture the life stories of the grandmothers we visited. Her story is remarkable and so fundamental to her character. Her spine is bending and her eyesight failing but she is still so strong, elegant and refined, with a masterfully dry sense of humour.

My memories of Lally and family centre around food. From Marmite and cucumber on toast with tea at 4 p.m. and shiny fish and chips on Devon beaches to the great Christmas Eve supper we have each year in tribute to her German family. At this meal there are at least three varieties of German sausage, carawayed sauerkraut and her special red cabbage cooked with grated apple and juniper berries. This is always served at a table with matching porcelain, 'Oma's' white linen tablecloth, copious white candles and red angel chimes. We are allowed one present. Everyone runs off to put something 'nice' on. I can picture her precision eye pencil now.

The scents, sounds, textures and the anticipation associated with this meal will never leave me. More than the food, it's the atmosphere that's created and the shared richness of family history. The gift of tradition is a marvellous thing.

Every grandmother we meet cooks something with context. They let us into their kitchens and memories so that we can capture the recipes and stories that risk being lost for ever.

—

Iska Lupton

MAKING GRAND DISHES

It began with our networks. We put feelers out, asked friends if they had a special grandmother we might be able to spend a day in the kitchen with. Soon enough, people got wind of what we were doing and started to reach out.

Travelling from the UK to Greece, France, Spain, Italy, Croatia, Poland and way further to Cuba, the USA, Mexico and Russia to cook with grannies of all ages, backgrounds and ethnicities for a weekend each time, we've picked up more than just culinary tips on our great gran mission.

The life experience that we've been gifted through this project is extraordinary. Leaving a grandmother's home after spending a day or weekend with her in her kitchen has become much like leaving our own grandmothers. They hug us tight and insist we come over again and we walk out with such warmth – in heart and belly. It is at these moments that we realise how important the project we've embarked on together is, picking up wisdom from women who know what it is to have truly lived.

We expected to pick up some good recipes doing *Grand Dishes*; we never could have imagined what we would learn about love, life and relationships. We have laughed hysterically and cried a lot. There have been grannies wearing pink wigs, chainsaw demonstrations, a whole tray of pasta bake dropped, a platter of peppers slipping off a granny's head and onto the floor. They give as good as they get. They tell us exactly what they're thinking.

There's an intimacy to be found in someone's kitchen. Invited into these grandmothers' homes for a weekend, from a Sicilian farm to a cacti-populated private island in Croatia, sharing simple tasks in a kitchen filled with the smells and flavours of a dish loaded with special memories, we form a bond with every woman we cook with.

That bond, quite naturally, has led to questions both of us have been churning over and over internally. 'How did you know when you'd met "the one"?' 'What makes a happy marriage?' 'How do you deal with grief?' and 'How does it really feel to be old?'

Both in our late 20s, we looked to these grandmothers for the answers we haven't lived long enough to give to each other. Open, willing and with so much wisdom, the answers came over a boiling pot, a finely chopped onion or a table creaking with the weight of the many dishes we'd set upon it. Their words are now sealed for ever in this book, along with the recipes that have seasoned these womens' lives.

They have changed the way we think, reminded us of the importance of looking forward, being kind, of love and legacy (be it through children, good deeds or special recipes) and that strange, shocking things could happen at any moment. Ultimately, that we should not worry so much about what we don't yet know, and just feast on life.

A NOTE ON RECIPES

A big learning: grandmothers do not use scales.
They just know. So we paused and measured and
tested so we could capture their recipes with as
much precision as possible, but the ingredients
may not be identical and some methodology slightly
unusual. We've provided both metric and imperial
measurements but recommend metric when baking
for ultimate precision.

We encourage you to use all your senses like they do,
to taste as you go and use your hands to really feel it.
This is how to learn by heart.

Amongst the stories and recipes, we've slotted
grandmother-inspired recipes and dedications from
special people in food across the globe. Receiving
these has been so fun, from Kathy Slack, who grew
up thinking 'hotpot' meant 'granny', to Anna Jones's
ultimate 'popping Yorkshires' and Francis Mallmann's
evocative account of his Uruguayan grandmother's
peach ice cream. Grandmothers really are such a
universal source of love and influence.

SOUPS

&

SIDES

MERCEDES

An unassuming lift in a 1970s apartment block opened on to a kaleidoscopic pattern-on-pattern-on-pattern apartment, where a petite woman of great character was poised to make *ajo blanco* soup with us. White garlic, white bread and white almonds against a house of red, pink, green and purple. A dainty, creamy, chilled soup produced by a grandmother who danced about her kitchen with extreme agility, spilling things and laughing endlessly. It was a splendid sensory onslaught from the moment we arrived.

At one point we asked what the tray on the wall was used for. It had a plate, cutlery and cups painted onto its surface in childlike strokes. 'Breakfast in bed – every day!' she told us. When we asked what that involved, she decided she'd perform it for us. Within 10 minutes she was sitting up under the covers in her pink-and-white nightie, spooning homemade marmalade onto toast.

We ate the soup from a giant porcelain soup tureen with a carnation strapped to the handle. This soup can be eaten immediately, but is better chilled for a couple of hours for the flavours to fuse. We took the time to fuse too, with a glass of red and a sliver of prosciutto. Then we all gathered around her *Vogue Living*-worthy dining table to dine on *ajo blanco* and *pimientos del pico rellenos de bacalao* (red peppers stuffed with cod), a dish from her childhood in northern Spain.

Born: *San Sebastián, Spain, 1931*
Mother tongue: *Spanish*
Grandchildren: *Coro, Carla, Mariana, Mariano, Enrique, Pedro, Juan, Jonás, Tomas, Mercedes, Ana, Isabela, Paloma*
They call her: *Abuela*

My family comes from the north of Spain, which is where this recipe comes from. In my home town of San Sebastián, the ladies of the house were supposed to cook very well, otherwise they were completely disgraced. If you didn't know how to cook very well, you were a pariah, so I had to learn not just to cook, but to do it well.

In my grandmother's house, which was really a temple of culinary knowledge, I learned absolutely everything I know now about cooking. We did everything at home, including slaughtering the animals we would eat. I remember watching bloody massacres of a chicken being placed between the cook's legs before being decapitated. Then it would run around the kitchen headless. I would then have to suffer seeing the entrails of the chicken being pulled out.

I thought it was the cabinet of horrors in my grandmother's kitchen. They'd put live lobsters on to boil and I would feel so awful about it, watching their claws being axed off. It was like torture. I hated it. I much preferred when I began to learn to cook in France during my summers in the Basque Country. It was less traumatic. When we would cook meat and fish there, it was already dead.

I actually had such a wonderful time in France when I was younger. Not just because the food was better, but because we were able to read books that were banned in Spain during Franco's rule. I'd spend hours consumed by Federico García Lorca. In fact, all the frivolous things we wanted, like fashion, were so much better in France than what we had access to here in Spain.

Franco found us a miserable nation after the war. There was nothing to eat and we had no clothes or shoes to wear, just hand-me-downs passed on from sister to sister. We'd buy meat on the black market from men who would carry around suspicious suitcases. They'd open them up and the suitcases would be packed full of all kinds of meat inside. No one farmed for the entire war period. There was no agriculture because everyone was out killing each other.

My grandmother however, had a lovely garden. When the war came, my mother, who was very practical, took away all her beautiful roses and flowers, and instead planted tomatoes, green beans, cabbages, carrots. I was inspired by this garden to begin using vegetables for centrepieces in my career as florist to the Spanish royals. Young married girls who want to have a lovely table can, for instance, use a wine-coloured centrepiece with red grapes, aubergines and mauve cabbage. Combined with different pinks, it looks lovely. Then the day after your party, you can eat all the vegetables.

I think giving birth is for cows, not for ladies. So when I was having my first boy I expressed the need for time to myself in the morning. My husband, who was really an angel, told me not to worry and that I could take my breakfast in bed. Ever since then, I have eaten my breakfast every morning in bed.

—

Abuela Mercedes

ABUELA MERCEDES'S SPANISH CHILLED ALMOND SOUP (*Ajo blanco*)

INGREDIENTS
(*Feeds 4*)

— 125g (4½oz) white bread,
  crusts removed (it's good to
  use up stale bread)
— 75g (½ cup) blanched almonds
— 1 large garlic clove,
  finely chopped
— 100g (3½oz) melon, cubed
  (Galia or honeydew work well)
— 1 tbsp red wine vinegar
— 100ml (7 tbsp) olive oil
— 1 egg
— 1 tsp salt
— 1 tbsp water
— handful fresh parsley,
  finely chopped

METHOD

1. Rip the bread into pieces and soak in water for 10 minutes.

2. Squeeze out the bread a little and add to a blender with the almonds, garlic, melon, vinegar, oil, egg, salt and water.

3. Blend for 4 minutes, until smooth and the consistency of single cream. Add more water, if needed.

4. Transfer into a bowl and put it into the fridge for at least 2 hours before serving into bowls with an extra drizzle of olive oil on top and a sprinkle of fresh parsley.

Tip: To get your soup colder quicker, a trick is to use iced water to blend.

ABUELA MERCEDES'S SPANISH ROASTED RED PEPPERS STUFFED WITH SALT COD
(*Pimientos del pico rellenos de bacalao*)

INGREDIENTS
(*Feeds 4*)

— 300g (10oz) salt cod, flaked
  by hand into small pieces
— 3 tbsp olive oil
— 3 onions, finely diced
— 2 garlic cloves, finely
  chopped
— 1 tbsp flour, plus extra
  for dusting
— 150ml (⅔ cup) milk
— 14 roasted red peppers
  from a jar (2 for the sauce)
— light olive oil for frying
— 1 egg, beaten
— 1 red pepper, finely chopped
— juice from the jar of peppers
— 50ml (scant ¼ cup) cream
— 350ml (1½ cups) fish stock
— handful fresh parsley,
  finely chopped

METHOD

1. To prepare for this dish you need to desalt the cod 24 hours in advance. Do this by soaking the flaked salt cod in a large bowl of cold water, changing the water every 6 hours if possible.

2. Heat 2 tbsp of the olive oil in a sauté pan and cook the onion for 5 minutes, then add the garlic and cook until everything is transparent, not golden – about 5 minutes more.

3. While the onions cook, drain the desalted cod (saving the water) and lay out on a clean tea towel to soak up any extra moisture. It's important that it's totally dry.

4. Set half the cooked onions and garlic aside in a bowl for the sauce. Spoon the cod into the onions, adding the remaining olive oil. Stir in ½ tbsp flour and a generous glug of the milk. Cook for 5 minutes as it thickens, then add the other ½ tbsp of flour and the rest of the milk. Cook for a further 5 minutes until the taste of flour has gone completely and it's a loose, slightly sticky béchamel consistency. Add a touch more milk if you think it's getting too thick.

5. Lay 12 of the peppers out on a tray or platter ready to stuff. Spoon about 1 tbsp of the cod mixture into each pepper and secure the top by threading a toothpick through.

6. Heat a deep frying pan with light olive oil about 2cm (¾in) high and prepare two wide bowls, one with flour in and one with beaten egg. Light olive oil is better, as extra virgin will smoke quicker due to its low burning point.

7. When the oil is frying hot (bubbles gather quickly round your wooden spoon when you dip the end in), begin to dip and coat each pepper first in flour and then in egg and drop into the hot oil.

8. Fry on each side until golden and remove with a slotted spoon onto a kitchen towel to remove excess oil. Keep warm while you make the sauce.

9. Put the saved bowl of cooked onion and garlic into a large saucepan on a medium heat. Add the 2 jarred peppers you saved, the chopped red pepper and a little juice from the pepper jar. Cook for 10 minutes until the peppers are soft and the mixture smells sweet.

10. Turn off the heat and use a hand blender to whizz the sauce together with the cream and fish stock.

11. Add the stuffed peppers to a pan with the sauce and cook on a low heat
    for 30 minutes before sprinkling with a handful of parsley and serving simply
    with a green side salad.

Babcia Ziuta's Polish Beetroot Soup (*Botwinka*)

Zuza Zak, food writer

Ingredients

— 2l (8 cups) water
— 1 bay leaf
— bunch *botwinka*, young beetroot with stalks and leaves, everything finely chopped
— 1 carrot, grated
— 1 parsnip, peeled and grated
— ½ celeriac, peeled and grated
— 1 fermented beetroot, cut into strips
— 250ml (1 cup) juice from the fermented beetroot
— 1 tbsp lemon juice
— 1 tsp caster sugar
— handful fresh parsley, finely chopped

Botwinka was the soup I left behind, in more ways than one. When writing my cookbook, *Polska: New Polish Cooking*, I left it out, as I felt I'd already had enough beetroot soup recipes for one book and I couldn't well leave out the main ones such as *borscht* and *chlodnik*. Yet this was the long-awaited soup of my childhood and one I would eventually come to miss once we moved to England.

We would only eat this soup in the springtime when the beetroot were very young. My grandma Ziuta would make a huge pan of it, so that the entire extended family (and any neighbours that happened to pop round) could have their fill for the whole year.

This soup is made with fermented beetroot and the juice. To ferment the beetroot, simply peel and chop it into strips, then place in a ceramic container and cover with warm water with a flat tablespoon of sea salt dissolved in it, a bay leaf, a few peppercorns and a few allspice berries. Leave this to ferment for four days at room temperature (completely immersed); on day five transfer into a sterilised jar and keep in the fridge.

Feeds 4

1. Cook all the vegetables, apart from the beetroot stalks and leaves, with the bay leaf for about 30 minutes in the water.

2. Add the chopped stalks and leaves and cook for a further 5 minutes on the lowest heat, then turn it off completely.

3. Add the fermented beetroot juice, lemon juice and sugar, and season with salt and pepper to your own taste.

4. Allow to stand for about 15 minutes, then serve with some sour cream and parsley on top.

GLORIA

It began with a mammoth drive - straight through the middle of the Brecon Beacons - to get to Gloria's farmhouse in Presteigne, on the border of England and Wales. A flat chunk of mist was sitting on the trees at the top of the valley; it had rained non-stop for the last 24 hours. This made the cosy inside of Gloria's barn conversion even more comforting. The house had touches of Colombia everywhere. Gloria's dish was a true extension of her - warm and bright with hidden depths and rich context.

Ajiaco is a Colombian staple. In Colombia they have a much greater array of potatoes with different flavour profiles. The recipe must combine potatoes that dissolve with potatoes that maintain shape, adding flavour and colour. In this recipe Gloria uses four kinds to mimic the variations found in traditional *ajiaco*. Ideally she would add a fifth variety - papa criolla - which have a deep yellow colour (and can be bought frozen in Colombian shops). The same goes for the traditional guascas (a native herb). She also tricks the eye and palate by adding fresh watercress for the illusion of fresh guascas. We finished with an elegant fruit-salad dessert of papaya, pineapple, orange, banana and grated coconut.

Born: *Medellín, Colombia, 1950*
Mother tongue: *Spanish*
Grandchildren: *Paloma, Santiago*
They call her: *Abuela*

I was a teenager when I first made this dish. I went to Bogotá in search of a different life and I went on my own. I was 17 years old and it was actually quite a scandal in my family because at the time, people stayed with their family until they married. I, on the other hand, had started saving to leave home aged 11.

I got a little room in a house with an old lady, Doña Carmensita. I was looking for accommodation, all alone in Bogotá, and I rented a room in her neighbour's house, which was like a cupboard, then she offered me a room in her home, which actually was much better and cheaper.

I ended up befriending Doña Carmensita. I'd do her shopping because she didn't walk very well. She was 78 years old when we first met and she was the one who introduced me to this dish. When she taught it to me, she would use

seven varieties of potatoes, but I like to use five. She would eat this on special occasions and would use the chickens that would sort of just run around in the yard.

Bogotá is high up in the mountains, so the climate is cold and this soup is so warming and lovely to have on a cold night. There's a lot of debate about the origins, but for me, it's a mix of indigenous cooking and Spanish influence. This one has so many different types of potatoes and maize, which are Colombian products. Potatoes and maize are new to Europe. We have something like 5,000 varieties in South America. And potatoes, if you have a refined taste for them, you can really notice the difference.

Carmensita was a very simple person with a simple house and a wood stove. At her table she had only two chairs: hers and mine. We would sit there and could easily pass three hours together.

She would tell me about her childhood and would give me advice without even giving me advice. She wasn't an educated person, but she had masses of wisdom. She also admired me. I left the comforts of home in Medellín for a dangerous world where I worked with street children who carried knives. We would really just sit and talk for hours. She would say to me, 'Talking is important and talking helps you get rid of what is bothering you.' It's no coincidence I became a psychoanalyst.

I think it's not the food itself but the sharing together that can heal you. It's very healing to sit at the table and discuss. The thinking of how my children are going to enjoy that dish and how we are all going to sit around and talk really is the driving force behind my cooking. And you know, the table really is an amazing place to resolve problems within families. You do it in a very informal, non-accusatory way. It also gives you space to pause and listen.

When my son died at the age of 21 in a traffic accident, I cooked and cried many times. I used to lay the table for him even when he wasn't there any more. He told me always, 'Mummy, never stop dancing or cooking.' It was a very hard time but so much of grief is being able to just be sad and admit, 'I feel this sadness because I loved this person and because I am alive.' If I didn't feel it, a part of me would not be alive any more. Me crying, me feeling sad is an expression of my humanity - not an expression of weakness. To be able to cry in a way that is healing and true to yourself actually requires a lot of strength.

I really believe that being optimistic, open to life, life experiences and what other people offer is what is important. It's important to receive what people have to give and to give back too - we get enriched when we give. Eating together brings in so much of this exchange, to feed a family, then for that family to engage and feed back in at the dinner table. It's like a life force that comes out. It doesn't have to be a complicated meal that you make. It's just the act of taking time off, to just sit together and converse.
—

Abuela Gloria

ABUELA GLORIA'S
COLOMBIAN CHICKEN, CORN
AND POTATO SOUP (*Ajiaco*)

INGREDIENTS

(Feeds 6)

— 1 celery stick, cut into large chunks
— 4 garlic cloves, 2 kept whole and
   2 chopped
— 1 red onion, half cut into large chunks
   and half diced
— 1 white onion, half cut into large
   chunks and half diced
— 1 large carrot, cut into large chunks
— 1 red pepper, cut into large chunks
— bunch spring onions, green tops only
— 4 corncobs (1 for the stock, 3 cut
   in half for each bowl of *ajiaco*)
— bunch fresh coriander, stalks only
— 1 whole chicken, or 6 chicken thighs
— 1 tbsp olive oil
— 1 baking potato, peeled and thinly
   sliced so it dissolves easily
— 800g (1¾lb) mixed small waxy
   potatoes, skin on and chopped into 1cm
   (½in) chunks (Gloria suggests Anya,
   Charlotte and red potatoes)
— handful dried guascas (optional,
   for authenticity)
— 2 handfuls watercress, torn

FOR THE SPICY AJÍ SAUCE

— bunch spring onions, white parts only,
   finely chopped
— bunch fresh coriander, leaves only,
   finely chopped
— 2 red chillies, finely chopped
— 1 large tomato, skin removed
   and chopped
— juice of ½ lime
— 2 tbsp white wine or cider vinegar

FOR THE GARNISH

— 6 tsp capers
— 6 tbsp sour cream
— 3 avocados, finely sliced

METHOD

1. Start by making the stock for the base of the soup: put the chopped celery, garlic, red and white onion chunks, carrots, red pepper and green ends of the spring onions into a pressure cooker or saucepan large enough to hold the veg and your chicken. Add one corncob (for extra corn flavour, says Gloria), the coriander stalks and chicken. Pour in enough water to cover, then season and feel free to chuck in any other rogue vegetables you need to use up to add more flavour.

2. Bring to a boil, then, if using a saucepan, put on the lid, reduce the heat and simmer for about 45 minutes until chicken is cooked through. If using a pressure cooker, put the lid on and cook for 20 minutes.

3. While the chicken is cooking you can prepare the *ají* sauce by combining all the ingredients listed in a bowl and top up with cold water to just cover.

4. When the chicken is done, turn off the heat and carefully remove it from the saucepan into a large bowl. When cool enough, shred the meat and set aside. Add the bones back into the broth and cook for a further hour.

5. Meanwhile heat the oil, fry the diced red and white onions for 10 minutes, until soft and golden. Put the shredded chicken and the fried onion in a sealable container with a ladle of the stock to keep them moist and put it in the fridge to marinate.

6. After 1 hour, remove the chicken bones and vegetables from the broth; they're no longer needed. Add the baking potato and cook for about 15 minutes until it starts to dissolve. Then add the rest of the potatoes, remaining corncobs and guascas (if using), and cook for a further 20 minutes. Taste for seasoning.

7. Take the shredded chicken from the fridge, add salt to taste and add to the pan to heat through.

8. Just before serving, stir in the ripped-up watercress and ladle into bowls, making sure each person gets a piece of sweetcorn. Put *ají* (for heat and acid), capers, sour cream and avocado on the table for everyone to add themselves as toppings.

Yiayia Elektra's Greek Chicken Soup with Egg and Lemon (*Avgolemono*)

James Ferguson, chef

Ingredients

— what remains of a
  roast chicken, with
  some meat left
— 1 garlic bulb, cut in half
— 2 carrots, peeled
— 1 medium onion,
  peeled and halved
— 2 celery sticks, cut in half
— 1 medium leek, washed,
  with the root and dark
  green part removed
— 1 generous handful long-
  grain rice or orzo pasta
— juice of 1 large lemon
— 3 eggs: 2 whole, 1 yolk

My grandma, Elektra, originally came from the island of Khios. Her family moved to Athens when she was a little girl. She met my grandfather (a Scotsman) during the war and they were married in Athens in 1946. After the war they moved to Leicester, where she raised her five children in a small house on a council estate.

She was a wonderful cook and recreated food from her homeland in ingenious ways. Cheshire cheese would replace feta and she'd strain yoghurt to make it more Greek. She never owned a chopping board and was seemingly able to chop any vegetable in mid-air.

She learnt to be thrifty. After a delicious roast chicken, absolutely nothing would be thrown away. Her delicious *avgolemono* (literally eggs and lemon) soup was a real family favourite. She taught the recipe to my own mother, who would make it for me and my brother.

The passing down of recipes through generations is very special. To my grandma, food represented love, and the act of producing a meal was a real expression of it. Consequently, my entire family on my father's side have a deep-rooted love of Greek cuisine. I often put her dishes on my menu and in a way, I think this makes her legacy live on.

Feeds 4

1. Strip the chicken of all leftover meat, saving the bones. Set the meat aside.

2. Place the carcass and bones in a saucepan in which they fit snugly and cover with water. Bring to the boil and skim off any scum that floats to the top.

3. Add all the vegetables (add a bit more water if necessary, to comfortably cover). Reduce to a simmer and allow to cook for about 1 hour.

4. Pass the broth through a sieve and place back on the heat. Keep all the vegetables except the garlic (it's done its job now) to one side and discard the carcass and chicken bones. Let the broth bubble and reduce a little to intensify its flavour. Now add the rice/orzo and simmer until cooked.

5. While the rice/orzo is cooking, chop the vegetables into nice soup-sized pieces, chunky or small (whatever size pleases you).

6. When the rice/orzo is ready, add the vegetables and chicken meat, and heat through.

7. In a bowl whisk the eggs, egg yolk and lemon juice. Take a ladleful of the soup and introduce it to the lemon and egg mixture, whisking constantly.

8. Now take the pan off the heat and pour the egg–lemon mixture into the broth and give it a good whirl until it's all incorporated.

9. Put the pan back on a low heat and bring it to just below boiling point (be careful, if the soup boils you will have pieces of scrambled eggs floating around!) to thicken it a little.

Grandmother Concordia Ramos Tapalla's Filipino Chicken Tinola Soup

Mary San Pablo, chef

Ingredients

- 4 tbsp coconut oil
- 400g (14oz) bone-in chicken thighs
- 1 onion, diced
- 3 garlic cloves, sliced
- 8 tbsp fish sauce
- 3 lemongrass sticks: 1 bruised, 2 sliced into thin rounds
- 80g (2¾oz) ginger, peeled and thinly sliced
- 4 chilli leaves (or 2 green chillies, pierced)
- 800ml (3⅓ cups) light chicken stock
- 100g (3½oz) green (young) papaya, cut into bite-sized pieces
- 100g (3 cups) moringa leaves or baby leaf spinach
- 2 pinches caster sugar

Hailing from a large family originating from the lowlands of Batangas in rural Philippines, my grandmother stuck close to her roots. Having helped in the paddy fields since she was knee-high, and growing bountiful produce in her family's backyard, she felt most at home surrounded by her greenery.

She provided for her own brood, of which my mother was one of eight, with produce from her unspoilt garden and vegetable patches. I spent summer vacations following her on her rounds through the bamboo trellises of snake beans and dainty branches of moringa. Then we would usually settle under the low-lying mango trees amongst her roaming chickens, and I would watch, mesmerised, as she would expertly toss the day's dried-out rice, dehusking with each wave she made.

Chicken Tinola is the sum of everything that surrounded my grandmother. It is served simply with jasmine rice and has a delicate hum of chilli and an abundant sense of comfort, as any traditional chicken soup would. This is a dish she would have in the pot in minutes; after a quick waltz around her garden and a turn in her kitchen, chicken and ginger would be elegantly wafting through the house. We would then sit back down and pluck at the moringa leaves, which would be added as a final flourish.

Feeds 4

1. Melt the coconut oil in a large pot then add the chicken, skin side down, and warm up gradually, allowing the chicken fat to gently render out.

2. Before the chicken begins to colour add the diced onion and garlic, and turn the chicken over with the skin now facing up. Cook out the onions and garlic until translucent, keeping the heat on low.

3. Season with half the fish sauce.

4. Add the remaining aromats; bruised lemongrass, ginger and chilli.

5. Add just enough chicken stock to cover and then keep on a constant simmer for 25–30 minutes. Skim off any impurities if they arise.

6. Halfway through cooking add the cut green papaya.

7. As this bubbles, pick moringa leaves (or get your baby spinach ready).

8. Once the chicken is cooked, taste and adjust the seasoning with more fish sauce and balance this out with a couple of pinches of sugar. This dish should be well rounded and savoury, aromatic and ever so slightly sweet.

9. Stir through the lemongrass and moringa or spinach, allowing the residual heat to wilt and draw out the flavours of these last ingredients.

HARRIET

What a blast we had here. New Orleans bursts with pride, and Harriet, like the rest of its citizens, is ablaze with love for her home. We were whisked into the New Orleans School of Cooking by mini Harriet, whose giant character far makes up for her stature. She barely breathed for us to get a word in edgeways, a double act with best bud Anne, who's also in the book (page 252). The pair didn't stop verbally sparring, Harriet kicking off when Anne dared make a comment about her roux.

It's no surprise the duo have made it onto US TV screens with their own cooking show. Whether it's debates on what differentiates a blonde roux from a white roux, to which vessel is best to use when adding spices, Harriet and Anne ping-pong their arguments across the kitchen. Back and forth, back and forth. They've made jolly fights about cooking into an Olympic sport.

Still, we were lifted by the way in which they buoyed each other. Harriet dominated conversation with endless stories but Anne, despite having heard them a hundred times before - 'Tell them about the time you took the train north that winter' - only encouraged the telling of them. A true example of what lifelong friendship can look like. Something we hope to one day embody ourselves.

Born: *New Orleans, Louisiana, USA, 1941*
Mother tongue: *American English*
Grandchildren: *Ben, Edward, Michael, Daniel, Katie Scarlett, Eli*
They call her: *Bobee*

This roux comes from the French influence on New Orleans, but the spices are from all over the world. It's the world in a pot. That's how New Orleans cooking is. We were a port of entry. Everybody met at the table and contributed.

I started cooking when I was 10 years old. My grandmother and mother taught me. I was an only child and they had to keep me real busy because without any siblings, I'd get into trouble. So if I didn't have baseball or track or basketball after school, then my mother would expect me to start the meals.

Back in the 1950s, the telephone would be a static one, so when my mother would call to check in on

me and make sure I was cooking dinner, I'd have to run across the living room and dining room to answer it. She'd then ask me how the food was doing, so I'd have to run right back to the kitchen to check on the food. Once when she called I burned the roux, so they got shrimp Creole without the roux for dinner. I've always enjoyed cooking but I don't like long things. A one-hour roux is never going to be on my agenda because I'm impatient with it. I just turn the heat up, stay with it and stir and stir and stir. My roux are done in 15 minutes.

Bisques are usually made for seafood. We're surrounded by water, so we eat a lot of seafood here. Halfway through this, you need to

check the flavour. You don't want it to taste like warm milk. So the key with cooking this is to keep tasting all the way through and if it needs it, you just have to add that flavour. If it's too milky, then we need salt. I use crab claw because it tastes of so much more.

I worked in a hospital for 24 years, supervising in the kitchen. I could never be on a hospital ward. I'm the kind of person that if you shed a tear, oh! I'm right there with you. So I stayed in the kitchen. It's tough work, hot work, dirty work. Artists make work in all types of mediums, but half of them have to die before people say, 'Oooh, how great he was.' When you work in food, you see people appreciating your art.

I didn't start my career as a TV cooking-show host until I was in my 70s. I retired, but I knew I couldn't stay at home. I was divorced at 50. He had another woman for 15 years. She was a friend of the family - supposedly. She would always come to our house. She came once for vacation with us. So things started adding up. I called one day and no one answered. So I got into my car and went to her house and there was his car. I confronted them but we stayed together another ten years before we divorced. It just wasn't the done thing.

I got a job before I divorced because I found out about the girl-friend and decided I would need to look after my kids when the

marriage ended. When the divorce finally happened what really hurt was my girlfriends ignoring me because their marriages weren't any better than mine. I was finally showing them, 'Hey, you can leave too,' and they didn't like it.

I had a period in which I just made friends with lots of gay guys. We would go to Mardi Gras together. They became my family and oh, it was so much fun. I made a new set of friends and I loved it. I am who I am today because of those friendships and experiences and hurts. You have to be prepared. You know yourself and you can do it. You don't know you have it, but that strength is inside of you.
—
Bobee Harriet

BOBEE HARRIET'S CORN AND CRAB BISQUE

INGREDIENTS
(Feeds 4-6)

— 1l (4 cups) chicken stock
— 2 garlic cloves, very finely chopped
— 2 bay leaves
— 1 tsp dried thyme
— 3 tbsp spice mix (equal parts cumin, dried oregano, paprika, salt, garlic powder, about 2 tsp each)
— pinch cayenne pepper
— 250g (1½ cups) frozen sweetcorn (or fresh sweetcorn, boiled and sliced from the cob)
— 2 spring onions, chopped
— 500ml (2¼ cups) single cream
— 200-250g (roughly 1 cup) crab meat (Harriet likes claw, but you can use any)
— glug of sherry (optional)
— handful fresh parsley, chopped

FOR THE ROUX

— 80g (5 tbsp + 1 tsp) butter
— 50g (6 tbsp) flour

METHOD

1. In a big soup pan combine the stock, garlic, herbs and spices with half the corn and bring to a simmer.

2. Meanwhile, in a separate pan make the roux. Melt the butter and slowly whisk in the flour and cook until it's lightly coloured.

3. Add the roux to the soup pan with the rest of the corn, followed by the spring onions (reserving a few to garnish), the cream and crab meat. Simmer gently for 5 minutes – the soup should thicken nicely. You can always add more water if you like the consistency a bit thinner.

4. Add a final dash of sherry, if you like, and serve into bowls topped with a sprinkle of parsley and the reserved spring onions.

Grandma Elsa's Austrian Chicken Dumpling Soup

Rachel Khoo, food writer and broadcaster

Ingredients

— 1.5l (6 cups) chicken stock
— 2 large carrots, roughly chopped
— 5 button mushrooms, thinly sliced
— ½ bunch fresh parsley, leaves chopped

For the dumplings

— 200g (7oz) raw chicken breast
— 100g (3½oz) white bread, crusts removed
— 100ml (7 tbsp) single cream
— 2 eggs: 1 whole, 1 yolk
— 1 tsp salt
— pinch cracked black pepper
— pinch nutmeg

My maternal grandma, who was from Austria, played a big part in my love for food. I have many fond memories of sitting in her small kitchen and watching her make delicious, hearty, home-cooked Austrian dishes. From apple strudel (she had a special strudel board to stretch out the dough) to the best chicken dumpling soup (perfect food when you're feeling under the weather). What I remember most of all from my grandma is the food was always supposed to bring people together and be joyful. That is something that has stuck with me ever since.

Feeds 4

1. Put the stock and carrots into a large pot. Bring the stock to a boil and boil for 10 minutes.

2. Meanwhile, put all the ingredients for the dumplings into an electric blender and whizz until you have a smooth paste. Form the paste into 20–25 dumpling shapes using 2 tablespoons (for smaller dumplings use 2 teaspoons).

3. Drop the dumplings into the boiling stock and cook for 5 minutes (3 minutes for the small ones), adding the mushrooms for the last minute.

4. When the dumplings are done, they will rise to the surface. Test for seasoning and then serve immediately, garnished with some roughly chopped parsley.

Recipe taken from *The Little Paris Kitchen* by Rachel Khoo

JUANA MARIA

Cubans have long been suffering from desperate food shortages, with people forced to wait for up to five hours a day to collect their rations of meat, poultry, eggs, rice, beans and other staples. The USA's blockade has catalysed the nation's most recent crisis, in which we met Juana Maria, who struggles daily to get by. Cuba's communist government regularly runs out of money to pay for food, two-thirds of which is imported. Hence the inflated costs at which we had to buy the few ingredients that make up this warming - but humble - plantain soup.

Juana Maria lives in a teeny-weeny flat on the outskirts of Havana. We took a 40-minute taxi ride - in an ancient 1950s Chevrolet - through streets pocked with potholes, past rainbow-coloured shanty houses and effervescent locals blasting salsa from their boomboxes in the street to get to her.

After whipping this up in her kitchen, which could barely squeeze two of us in, we sat down in the living room, crammed with bric-a-brac and religious icons, and tucked into our soup. Somehow Juana Maria had managed to turn just three ingredients - a plantain, chicken stock and an onion (she adds Gouda when she can find it) - into a delicious, hearty meal. We were even more surprised to hear the role her husband had had in *la Revolución Cubana*, and sat like children at story time, handling her ration book and listening to her recount the first days of Che Guevara and Fidel Castro's revolution in La Habana.

Born: *Matanzas, Cuba, 1934*
Mother tongue: *Spanish*
Grandchildren: *Gillian Alejandra, Kevin Eloy*
They call her: *Abuela*

I began to make this soup around 40 years ago because I don't like noodles with soup or pasta in a broth, so I decided to start adding plantain to make my broth more substantial. The traditional plantain soup in Cuba is usually a broth with bits of plantain included, but I just took out the bits I didn't like and added more plantain. The original version is chicken stock, potatoes, sweet potatoes or noodles.

I was born in Matanzas, so I'm a country girl. I came to Havana in 1952 when my godparents invited me here. I was 18 and a city life called to me. I had so many siblings and my mother was very authoritarian, so when I moved to Havana with my wealthy godparents, life improved. It meant freedom.

I went to learn shorthand and to type, then I became a hairdresser and manicurist. The opportunities were here.

At that time, everyone was aware of a revolution brewing. I came to Havana in the very same year that the leader of the opposition to President Batista's regime killed himself - supposedly. We all knew that if you took part in these things, you could be killed. If you didn't, then you'd be left alone. I never took part. My husband, however, was one of the original revolutionaries. He took part in the famous attack on the presidential palace in 1957. We were not married yet, but we were together. I was working at the hair salon and he came to give me a message that something would happen at 3 p.m. I didn't know where and on what scale. He said, 'If you don't see me again, it's because tomorrow, something will happen.'

Many people were killed during Batista's time. We would hear about arrests, torture and murder. This was frequent and we all would know someone who knew someone who'd been taken. He was a corrupted man, in cahoots with the American mafia. They owned Cuba. It was such a charged time to live through.

On the day of the triumph of the revolution, my husband and I were on a bus from Havana to Matanzas to celebrate New Year at my parents' home. I didn't know anything had happened. It was only when we arrived in Matanzas that we learned Fidel Castro and Che Guevara had overthrown Batista. It was 1 January 1959. My husband decided we should get back to Havana immediately, but the revolutionary soldiers shot the tyres of the bus flat to prevent any uprising against the revolution.

It took three full days to walk all the way back to Havana. My husband was so desperate to get back to to celebrate the revolution. I was furious with him for making me walk, and he was elated. No bad mood of mine could bring him down, though. He was married to the revolution.

Those first years were glorious. The new laws greatly benefited the people. The land and housing reforms meant that everyone had a roof over their heads. Evictions were not a thing and homelessness ended. Also, everything was suddenly very cheap. You paid 40 cents for a litre of milk. The sheen faded fast, though. Before the revolution, Cuba was plentiful. Stores are empty now.

I've had my ration book since the early days of the revolution, but what we have access to has fluctuated over the years. The list was long before the crisis of 1990. We could have potato paste, detergent, soap, animal fat to cook with, beef. Now it's 7lbs of rice, 3lbs of sugar, 10 ounces of beans, 1 packet of coffee for the month, 8 ounces of oil per month and 1.75lbs of chicken. It's basically just the meat off the chicken without the skin, bones or fat. Then the man selling it to you will steal a part of it for himself.

It isn't the prices that went up but a severe scarcity of food, because the government can't afford to pay workers to produce food here in Cuba and we have this embargo from America which makes importing from there impossible. My neighbours keep chickens in their tiny apartments here in Havana, just to have a couple of eggs each week.

Now to cook, you have to go through the black market. That's things that have fallen off trucks, things that have been stolen, or perhaps the odd fish or lobster that has been smuggled into the city from the periphery.

Getting out isn't so easy for me any more. I can't stand in a queue for three hours for a piece of chicken, which is what most people have to do to get their hands on ingredients every day.

Things like onions and tomatoes are at ridiculous prices. It was 5 CUC (convertible pesos) for some onions and tomatoes just for this meal today. That's basically $5. So far, my daughters and grandchildren are helping me. Otherwise I would not be able to survive with what the government hand out.

In order to live decently in Cuba, you either have to have it very hard or be born into a wealthy family with connections. When my daughters' children were born, they were the happiest moments of my life, but being a grandmother, for me, is about teaching them to survive and to do everything they can in order to get by in this world.
—

Abuela Juana Maria

ABUELA JUANA MARIA'S CUBAN PLANTAIN SOUP

INGREDIENTS
(Feeds 6)

— 1 chicken carcass
  (fresh from the butcher
  or left over from a roast)
— 1.5l (6 cups) water
— 1 onion, peeled and
  quartered
— 3 garlic cloves, peeled
  and bashed
— 3 unripe green plantains,
  peeled and sliced into
  3mm (⅛in) rounds
— 600ml (2½ cups) vegetable
  oil, for deep frying (or
  follow the option to bake)
— 200g (1¾ cups) Gouda,
  grated
— handful fresh coriander,
  chopped

METHOD

1. In a large pot, put the chicken carcass, water, onion and garlic. Bring to the boil and then simmer on a low heat for about 40 minutes.

2. While your broth is simmering, tend to your plantains. You want to make sure they are nice and green; this means they won't be too sweet and will be super-starchy inside – perfect for thickening the soup. Your slices should be thin (don't be tempted to slice fatter than 3mm/⅛in), as the aim is to deep-fry or bake them so they are really crispy, then blend them into a powder.

3. To deep-fry: heat the oil in a pan suitable for deep-frying and then fry the plantain rounds in batches, ensuring your oil is sizzling hot before the plantain goes in. Take care not to overcrowd the pan or let the pieces touch each other. After about 6 minutes, or when the plantain is deep golden brown all over, remove with a slotted spoon and place on a kitchen towel to soak up the excess oil. Repeat until all the plantain is done. Allow the slices to cool – they should be nice and crisp.

4. To bake: preheat oven to 200°C/180°C fan/400°F/gas 6, and lay the rounds out on a couple of lined baking trays. Pop them in the oven for around 15–20 minutes or until they've lifted from the sheet at the edges and turned pale with touches of light brown. Remove from the oven and allow to crisp up as they cool.

5. Reserve a few for decoration and then crush the plantain slices to a powder using a spice grinder or blender, or if you're feeling strong like Juana Maria, in a pestle and mortar. You may have to do it in a couple of batches. Pulse and scrape down the sides until it reaches a sandy texture.

6. Once your broth is ready, discard the onion, garlic and chicken. Add your crushed plantain to the broth and stir until the soup thickens. Season to taste, and if you like your soup a bit thinner, add a little more water.

7. As a final touch, you can add grated Gouda and top with a sprinkling of fresh coriander and the crispy plantain you set aside earlier.

Grandmother Lusia's Ukranian Gherkin, Pork and Buckwheat Soup (*Rassolnik*)

Olia Hercules, chef and food writer

For the stock

— 500g (1lb) well-marbled
    pork ribs
— 1 onion, peeled and
    roughly chopped
— 2 sticks celery,
    roughly chopped
— 1 carrot, peeled and
    roughly chopped
— 1 bay leaf
— 5 peppercorns
— 5 allspice berries

For the broth

— 100g (½ cup) buckwheat,
    pearl barley or rice
— 2 tbsp sunflower oil
— 3 shallots, peeled and diced
— 1 carrot, grated
— 100g (3½oz) gherkins,
    peeled and grated
— 200ml (¾ cup + 2 tbsp)
    gherkin brine
— 1 tbsp fresh dill, chopped

This soup, called *rassolnik*, is my grandmother Lusia's dish. She was both strong and gentle, a mother of six and an incredible cook. The meat needs to have a good amount of fat on it, as this is the whole point of using gherkins – they cut through the fat beautifully. You should only use brined gherkins, as even the nicest vinegar will spoil this dish. Look for a label with *ogórek kwaszony* in Polish or Eastern European shops. It does not take long to make this soup once the stock is done: you can make stock in advance and freeze it. It is hearty and nourishing, a meal in itself.

Feeds 4

1. Place the meat into a large saucepan and cover with 2.5l (2¼ quarts) cold water. Add the onion, celery, carrot, bay leaf, peppercorns and allspice and bring to the boil.

2. Lower the heat as soon as the water boils and skim any scum from the surface.

3. Simmer for a couple of hours while you watch your favourite series and eat gherkins.

4. When the meat is tender and falling off the bone, add your grain and cook for 15 minutes or until cooked but still has a bite.

5. Meanwhile, sweat the shallots in the oil for 5 minutes and then add the carrot and cook over a medium–low heat, stirring often until everything is soft and starting to caramelise slightly.

6. Then add the gherkins, taste the broth and add half of the gherkin brine. Taste it and add more if you think it needs more salt. The broth should taste rich but also a little salty, sweet and sour. Serve with fresh dill and a huge hunk of good bread.

ZENA

We know Zena's granddaughter Olivia. She was there when we arrived at Zena's Hampstead flat, and they'd gone for a coordinating white shirt with black-ribbon-necktie 'look'. It was like walking in on a couple of excitable 15-year-olds. We began with tea and biscuits, as is traditional, and quickly got on to the subject of exercise. Zena made the giant claim that she can hold a plank for 300 counts. A few counts later she was on the floor with a cushion under her elbows, proving that small people can indeed have extraordinary strength of core (and mind).

Her flat was impeccably presented. China was placed with precision and every cushion plumped to the max on the big cream sofa, which almost engulfed her when she sank into it for her portrait. She cooked with a choreography of small, delicate movements, as if her hands were barely touching the ingredients. Then out came these bold snacks, which we ate while warm, and quickly lost count of how many we'd had.

We never push grandmothers to do a recipe that isn't intrinsically connected to them, so we were very happy to go with Zena's take on *piroshkis* (more a turkey sausage roll than traditional *piroshki*). But when she told us the secret to the sneaky version of the sauce – a mix of ketchup and brown sauce – we did have to ask her to share her more elaborate 'homemade' version. You choose which one to use.

Born: *South Africa, 1929*
Mother tongue: *English*
Grandchildren: *Brett, Olivia, Lauren, Samantha*
They call her: *Mama Zene*

The most esteemed guest to have eaten my *piroshkis* at a luncheon was Margaret Thatcher, who was perfectly charming. This recipe goes back very far. My mother was Russian and she taught me. She was just 10 years old when she left Russia, so this was probably her way of holding on to her heritage. When we would have dinner parties, everyone wanted the recipe, but because it's so simple, I was embarrassed to pass it on.

My cooking is simple, but it's always healthy and tastes delicious. There's no question that the key to keeping youthful is to eat well and exercise. I have chronic leukaemia, but I don't even think about it. My granddaughter bought me a Pilates DVD and I learned it by

heart so that I can do the exercises every morning, from anywhere. I can hold a plank for 300 counts.

I never think of myself as my actual age. I used to see people that were 80 and think, Oh God, are they old! But here I am at my age and I really do think young. I've had a very active life. In South Africa my first business was a butcher's shop (at my father's suggestion). I remember walking in for the first time, seeing all this sawdust and blood on the floor. The man we bought it from was awful. He told everyone I was Jewish – in such an anti-Semitic area – because he wanted to sabotage our business, but I persevered and made a great success of it. I wanted to leave South Africa though, so we sold the business and my husband put the money into a trust fund his friend had set up. The night before I was due to fly to London with the children, we went for dinner at his parents' house. I could see he was anxious, puffing away at his cigarettes. I asked his mother what was the matter with him and she said, 'You don't know? You've lost all your money.' Well, I could have murdered that man there and then. I worked day and night for three years for that money and he lost it all.

We borrowed money for the flight and got a one-room apartment with beds that folded into the wall. I was just so happy to be out of South Africa and to be seeing trees for the first time that I made it work. I went to college and did a course in hair and beauty, then the same college asked me to teach my own course. Then Revlon got to hear about me and I began working with them, travelling all over doing their promotions.

When my husband died I thought the end of my life had come. I started playing golf to distract myself and I met Murray there. I was with him for 15 years until I met Jerry, my current companion. He's a rocket scientist – Jerry put the first American into space.

I met him while I was holidaying in Florida. I was actually with Murray at the time. We had a pleasant relationship but nothing special. When I went out with Jerry I felt I'd known him all my life. There was such a connection, I couldn't get over it. I asked him if he'd like to join me for the weekend in Palm Beach and he said, 'Sure.' I'd just met him! He came over and we spoke for hours. And Murray was at home in London and was supposed to come to Palm Beach to join me that weekend too. I phoned him and told him, 'Murray, don't come. I've fallen in love.' I was in my 70s.

—

Mama Zene

MAMA ZENE'S RUSSIAN TURKEY ROLLS (*Piroshkis*)

INGREDIENTS
(*Makes 20*)

— 1 medium onion,
 finely diced
— 1 tbsp coconut oil
— 300g (10½oz) turkey mince
— 1 x 320g (11½oz) pack ready-
 rolled puff pastry
— 1 egg, beaten (to glaze)

FOR THE TOMATO SAUCE

— 200g (7oz) tinned chopped
 tomatoes (half a tin)
— 1 tbsp soft brown sugar
— 1 tbsp tomato purée
— 2 tbsp balsamic vinegar
— 2 tbsp Worcester sauce

FOR THE QUICKER, SNEAKY SAUCE

— 3 tbsp tomato ketchup
— 3 tbsp HP or other
 brown sauce
— handful fresh coriander,
 chopped

METHOD

1. Preheat oven to 200°C/180°C fan/400°F/gas 6.

2. In a pan, combine the tomato sauce ingredients. Break down the tomatoes with a fork and reduce down to a ketchup consistency for about 10 minutes. Add salt and pepper to taste.

3. Meanwhile, fry the chopped onion in the coconut oil until browning and then add the mince, stirring and breaking up the meat with a wooden spoon until cooked through.

4. Add all the sauce to the mince and stir together (or seasoned ketchup and brown sauce, if you're cheating). Put aside to cool.

5. Lay your piece of ready-rolled puff pastry on a lightly floured surface. Slice it in half lengthways.

6. Take one half of the pastry and place half of the mince mixture neatly along one of the long edges, leaving a 1cm (½in) gap between the filling and the edge of the pastry.

7. Brush the 1cm (½in) edge with a little water (Zena uses an ice cube!) to help it stick.

8. Fold the opposite edge over and around the meat, tucking under slightly, to meet the moistened side. Squeeze slightly to ensure the pastry is stuck and the meat is enclosed. Roll the pastry over so the seam is underneath.

9. Cut into 10 pieces (around 3cm/1¼in each) and place on a floured baking tray.

10. Repeat with remaining pastry and mince, and brush the top of each roll with egg wash.

11. Bake in the oven for 20 minutes until golden on top. Serve with a glass of bubbles.

HELEN

We drove two hours from Nashville to Helen's in Brownsville to catch her in pre-lunch preparation mode. On a very grey day we drove through the middle of endless cotton fields; spiky brown branches with bright white tops, a little darkness lingering behind their fluffy exterior.

Helen's 'Bar-B-Que' is operated from a 100-year-old dark red wood-panelled shed in the middle of a parking lot. She's one of the few female pit-cooks in the country and by lunchtime trucks were whipping into the lot for her pulled pork and coleslaw, baloney sandwiches and beans. What looked like the smoking remnants of an arson attack was actually Helen's pit room, built onto the back of the shed. The room was entirely filled with smoke; you couldn't see 30cm (1ft) in front of you and we were all crying immediately, Helen with a little more composure.

Inside resembled a David Lynch set; dark wood veneer and daylight filtering through dust to land on the ketchup and salt. Helen was behind the serving hatch, pushing white cabbages through the blender with a characteristic grit.

Various family members came through the kitchen swing door during the morning: her niece, to ask for money (to no avail); her cousin, to peel potatoes in exchange for a can of Coke; her daughter, to serve at the hatch for a bit. The meat was smoky and delicious, paired with her signature sauce. There was a mild or spicy barbeque sauce, and we were absolutely not allowed to know the recipes for these.

Born: *Brownsville, Tennessee, USA, 1955*
Mother tongue: *American English*
Grandchildren: *Makeeva, Arion, Andre, Shay, Jordan, Deshia, Deshawn, Ashton*
They call her: *Grandma*

I've been developing a top-secret BBQ sauce recipe for 20 years. I can't disclose that at all, but you're welcome to my beans, coleslaw and potato salad. I've been here for 23 years. I never cook at home. I just cook at my barbecue smokehouse.

Here I have all my contraptions and various slicers, so that things happen much faster than people would expect them to. I have so many different gadgets to chop down my carrots real fine and cube my peppers extra tiny to

add to the beans. I just have gotten used to this place and so it's here that I do all of my cooking. I'll probably be here until the day I die.

I used to work for the previous owners in this same ol' spot. I worked for them for 15 years making sandwiches, until they passed it on over to me. It used to be a garage before it was a BBQ smokehouse and would you believe, this rickety old shack is almost 100 years old?

This has basically become my home. I just live here and I just love it and I love my customers. All of them are so sweet. I don't have any problem at all out of my customers. My family are always in and out too. It's a family affair here – my granddaughters come all the time to help me out. They're the only customers I get any hassle from. Nieces, nephews – all of them – they come down here when they need a little loose change, if you know what I mean. I end up helping all of them and cussing them at the same time.

I was real young when I had my first kid. I was only 18 and I just got stupid. I didn't even like his daddy. My current husband and I have only one child together, but I have a lot of grandkids. My son seems to be planting kids all over the world. He got them here and he got them there. He has a set of twins by one girl. Then he got another boy by another girl, then he got two girls by another girl. I do warn these women, but they don't take any heed. 'He doesn't take care of these babies,' I say, but these girls don't listen to me. He certainly won't ever listen to me. He's just very charming and I'm proud of him for that, at least. With children and grandchildren, you can try and tell them, but if they don't want to listen, they just won't and it's our job as a parent or grandparent to just accept that you have done your best.

As a grandmother, I'm doing all the things that the mother ain't doing. I have raised two of my grandkids. I raised the two girls, Andre and Shay. I could see they needed it and so I stepped up. That's your role if your kids can't take it on.

I don't think I'm going to be retiring any time soon. As long as I have my health, I'll just keep going. The key for me is to just keep on at it and I'll be as young as I feel. The arthritis doesn't help, but being occupied keeps me young. I can't be as quick as I used to be because I have arthritis in my hands and my knees. There's absolutely nothing you can do at all for arthritis, apart from hurt.
—

Grandma Helen

GRANDMA HELEN'S SOUTHERN BBQ SIDES

INGREDIENTS
(*Feeds 4*)

FOR THE BAKED BEANS

— 1 tbsp olive oil
— 1 small onion, finely diced
— 4 rashers streaky bacon, finely diced
  (Helen uses offcuts of pulled pork)
— 1 green or red pepper, finely diced
— 2 x 400g (14oz) tins pinto beans,
  drained
— 1 x 400g (14oz) tin chopped tomatoes
— 1 tbsp brown sugar
— 2 tbsp Worcester sauce
— 1 tsp salt
— 1 tsp smoked paprika

FOR THE COLESLAW

— ½ white cabbage, finely shredded
— 1 large carrot, shredded or grated
— 100g (scant ½ cup) mayonnaise
— 2 tsp yellow mustard
— 1 tbsp white wine vinegar
— 1 tsp caster sugar

FOR THE POTATO SALAD

— 1 egg
— 500g (1lb) waxy potatoes, peeled
  and cubed
— 1 stick celery, finely chopped
— 5 small gherkins (or 2 big),
  finely chopped (plus some juice)
— 80g (5 tbsp) mayonnaise
— 1 tsp yellow mustard
— 3 spring onions (optional)

METHOD

1. To make the beans: preheat oven to 190°C/170°C fan/375°F/gas 5. Heat oil in an ovenproof casserole over a medium-high heat. Sauté the onion for 5 minutes until it begins to soften, not brown.

2. Add the bacon and diced pepper and cook and stir until bacon is browned, 7–10 minutes more.

3. Tip in the beans, tomatoes, sugar, Worcester sauce, salt and smoked paprika. Transfer the pot to the oven with the lid on and bake until bubbling and browned, about 1½ hours. Return to the top of the stove and reduce without the lid until sticky and resembling baked beans as we know! While they cook, prepare your slaw and potato salad.

4. To make the slaw: combine the cabbage and carrot in a large bowl. In a separate small bowl or jar, mix the mayo, mustard, vinegar, sugar and a pinch of salt to make the dressing. Pour over the cabbage and carrot and pop in the fridge until needed.

5. To make the potato salad, put the egg on to hard boil, about 8 minutes. Once the egg is done, remove with a slotted spoon and run under the cold tap. Keep the egg pan boiling and add the potatoes for 7-8 minutes, or until tender. Drain the potatoes and place in a mixing bowl.

6. Peel and finely chop the egg and add to the bowl of potatoes, followed by the celery and gherkins.

7. Mix the mayonnaise and mustard together with 1 tbsp gherkin juice in your dressing bowl or jar. Pour over the potato mixture and stir gently but thoroughly to combine. Add spring onion if you like. Keep in the fridge until needed.

8. When the beans are ready, serve with the slaw and potatoes and partner with pulled pork and BBQ sauce.

EDNA

In Tel Aviv we revelled in *shakshuka*, dunking thick *challah* bread into runny egg yolks and tomato stew rich with cumin daily. We marvelled at the city's rich culinary scene. It's a paradise for food lovers. It's also a city of contradictions in which we were made to feel so welcome by those who once were strangers to the place themselves. It's a place laden with expectations and heavy with judgement. And so we went into Edna's city apartment armed with questions about what it really feels like to be a 'citizen' of Israel. How do those who migrated here perceive their own relationships and claim on this rich city?

The door opened on to a cosy apartment, framed photographs of grandchildren lining the walls and an entire family – Edna, her husband, her granddaughter Shira and her son and daughter-in-law – to welcome us in from the blustery day beyond this warm scene.

We were given a quick demo on how to make her super-simple marinated peppers, to be served as a side or as part of a table full of meze sharing-style plates. Most of our time with Edna was spent chatting about the city and her husband, who she's still goo-goo eyed over so many years into their marriage. The whole experience felt so wholesome against a backdrop of extreme contention. It made us realise just how complex and contradictory humans really are.

Born: *Bucharest, Romania, 1931*
Mother tongue: *Romanian*
Grandchildren: *Shira, Maayan, Rotem, Yuval, Amit, Itsan, Hagar, Neta, Adili, Ido, Boaz, Brit*
They call her: *Sabta*

This is a dish I like to make because it's simple, easy and instantly reminds me of my childhood growing up in Romania. It's usually something we will eat as a starting dish or as an accompaniment to a main meal and it's really very typically Romanian. We can use green and yellow peppers too for this – I just chose red for today.

We didn't like it so much in Romania because we were Jews and it was a hard time because of the war. I was just a little girl when we left for Palestine, towards the end of the Second World War. When we arrived it suddenly struck me that everyone

was Jewish. It was nice to finally belong. Nobody was going to call us names or be racist towards us.

In Romania we suffered a lot of prejudice, even being from a good family. My father had a factory for printing silk and we were less endangered than other Romanian Jews, because we were from a well-to-do family. It was when we were moved from our mixed school to an all-Jewish school that I began to notice the changes that were happening around me. I was just a girl, but it was impossible to ignore the names that they would call us. So I wasn't afraid of leaving Romania, but I was sorry about leaving my friends. It was lucky that we were young and could actually adapt to a new life and culture.

I can crochet, I can sew, I do ceramics, I can make shoes, I paint and do glazing and enamelling – I'm very into crafting and I've taken many courses. I knit almost every day. I can't live without doing something. It may be what keeps me going. I think my husband is another reason I feel young. I met him when I was 17 on a kibbutz, which is basically a commune we'd gone to work on for the summer. I had this old camera I'd had since I was 12 and he made the first move by asking if he could play with it. I gave it to him and he played with it for ages, but I didn't mind because I liked him. I still have the camera, actually.

At the kibbutz we were put in the same group and the sleeping arrangements were very relaxed. Boys and girls all slept in the same room together, so on the first day he asked me, 'Where do you want to sleep?' I said, 'I don't mind.' So then he responded, saying, 'Maybe you sleep there and I sleep here, then?' and pointed to two beds next to each other. And so we did. We didn't touch at all but the whole time I could feel he was next to me.

No one believes how in love we are all these decades later. I love him exactly as I did when I was young. He's a special man. He's just something out of this world. I don't know what the secret is, but we never parted. I still want to embrace him and to kiss him. We are in very good relations. All I know is that if you don't compromise, you don't move forward. You must also look for an honest man that loves you. You just feel it. I can't explain it in words, but the feeling sticks to you. I really do love him today like I loved him the first day.

The most important thing in life is to have good relations with people, which isn't easy. Everyone has their own character, but we can't depend on only ourselves. It's hard here because it will never be a love story between the Palestinians and the Jews. It feels like it has been like this a long time, but we are trying to live together peacefully and not be fighting all the time.

—

Sabta Edna

SABTA EDNA'S ROMANIAN PICKLED PEPPERS

INGREDIENTS

(Feeds 4 as part of a meze)

— ½ tsp olive oil
— 2 large red peppers
— apple cider vinegar
— pinch sea salt
— pinch granulated sugar

METHOD

1. Take a drop of oil in your hand and rub all over the two peppers. Place the two peppers directly onto the gas hob or under the grill on the highest setting and begin to blister the peppers.

2. Use tongs to turn the peppers once one side is charred. Keep cooking until the skin of the whole pepper is black; this could take up to 15–20 minutes.

3. When done, place the peppers in a glass bowl with a plate or cling film over the top for 5–10 minutes to loosen the skin.

4. When the time is up you should be able to rub all the black skin off with your hands – it's OK if a few flecks are left. Cut around the stalk to remove the heart and seeds, then lay out on a board and sprinkle all over with a little salt and sugar.

5. Put in a wide bowl and just cover with apple cider vinegar and leave at room temperature for 1 hour.

6. When the time is up, pour away the vinegar (save for a dressing if you like) and serve the peppers as part of a meze feast with cheeses and salamis.

Yiayia Maria's Greek Carrot Fritters (*Keftedes*)
Maria Elia, chef

Ingredients

— 350g (12oz) carrots
— 2 tbsp olive oil
— 1 small onion, grated
— 150g (⅔ cup) feta, crumbled
— 50g (1 cup) fresh breadcrumbs
— 1 tsp cinnamon
— 2 tsp dried mint
— 50g (scant ½ cup)
  parmesan, grated
— 10g (2 tsp) fresh flat-leaf
  parsley, finely chopped
— 1 egg, beaten
— plain flour, to dust
— olive or vegetable oil,
  for shallow frying

One of my earliest childhood memories is eating *keftedes* with my Yiayia. My grandma came over from Cyprus to help my dad in his restaurant. I used to get involved at the age of four helping out with minor tasks such as feeding potatoes through the rumbler and grating Kefalotyri cheese. It's where I found my passion for cooking.

Normally *keftedes* are made with minced meat (they're basically meatballs). These vegetarian alternatives are packed with flavour. Pre-roasting the carrots brings out their natural sweetness, which is balanced by the salt-sour feta. Mint and parsley add freshness, with a hint of cinnamon for spice. These *keftedes* are just as delicious served cold. This is my vegetarian version of these Greek meatballs, dedicated to my Yiayia Maria.

Feeds 4, makes 16

1. Preheat oven to 200°C/180°C fan/400°F/gas 6.

2. Peel and top and tail the carrots, and leave whole. Drizzle with the olive oil, place in a roasting tin and cook for 30–40 minutes (depending on the size of carrots) until al dente, turning them halfway through. Leave to cool.

3. Grate the carrots into a bowl and mix with the rest of the ingredients, except the flour and oil. Season with sea salt and freshly ground pepper and refrigerate for 1 hour. (The mixture can be made the day before and refrigerated until required.)

4. Shape into 16 walnut-sized balls and dust in flour. You can either shallow fry them in olive oil or deep-fry them in vegetable oil. If using olive oil, heat in a frying pan over a medium heat, add half the *keftedes* and fry until golden on either side – about 3 minutes. Repeat with the remaining balls.

5. If using vegetable oil, deep-fry the *keftedes* for about 3 minutes at 180°C (350°F) until golden. Drain on kitchen paper and serve warm.

DORA

Dora is the head chef at Rocca Delle Tre Contrade, an elegant villa encircled by lemon groves, standing on a hill between the Ionian Sea and Mount Etna, where Iska spent a summer cooking with her. Dora is well under five feet tall, her perfectly fluffed hair adding an inch or two. She wears little heeled sandals while cooking and commands her kitchen with a booming, husky voice.

She serves four immaculate courses every evening for 24 adoring guests, twisting *spaghetti alla vongole* in a ladle and onto plates, lifting the weight of a whole suckling pig from the oven and carving like a master butcher. She measures everything by hand, seasons with abandon and tastes constantly until she is happy. She frequents the fish market in Giarre at 7 a.m., where they fear her, for she can be satisfied with only the freshest, finest fish.

Her dishes are intrinsically Sicilian with modern flourishes. This *caponata* - sweet and sour in equal measure, sticky with a varnish of olive oil - is served once a week as an aperitivo and devoured by the guests. It's best served warm but is also delicious cold from the fridge the next day, when the flavours have deepened. Dora uses a deep-fat fryer to brown all the peppers and aubergines before they're added. You can simply brown in olive oil.

Born: *Giarre, Italy, 1953*
Mother tongue: *Italian*
Grandchildren: *Laura, Sofia*
They call her: *Nonna*

I've been cooking for a long time. When my mother came back to Sicily from Australia she opened a casual restaurant and I went to work with her, which was the first time I worked in a professional kitchen. We made *arancini, pasta al forno*, rotisserie chicken... It was the first restaurant of its kind in Giarre.

My mother was a businesswoman; she was very clever and hard-working but everything I learned about being a good cook came from my grandmother. She cooked with passion and it was always completely effortless. I remember the smell of her making bread and *Pan di Spagna*. Everything was home-made at our house.

My grandmother was a remarkable woman. Fifteen days after her youngest child was born, my grandfather died, so she was left alone with six children. The first thing she did was sell all the bedsheets. When couples marry in Sicily it's traditional that the family prepare the *corredo* - or kit - for them: towels, pillows, sheets and things. After she sold her own, she started buying and selling more and more and turned it into a business. She did lots of research to find the best suppliers and embroiderers. She was entrepreneurial, a quality she likely passed on to my mother.

I lived with her from the age of three months old, and she raised me, more so than my own mother. When I was eight years old my mother left to live in Australia, where she worked at a restaurant opened by my uncle. There was no money to be made in Sicily at that time and many people left Sicily for America, Australia or Germany. So she left me with my grandmother and didn't return until I was practically a grown woman - 17 years old.

I was also separated from my sister because my mother took her to Australia. My sister was younger than I was and so it was decided that she'd be the one to go with my mother. We didn't become close until later in life, after we were both married.

In those days, when girls in Sicily finished school, they went to study stitching in a religious institute, which is what I did. Shortly after I fell in love with my husband. I was only 16 when we fell in love and it didn't take long to walk down the aisle. I was 17 on my wedding day.

I liked him because he was so funny and kind. We can laugh together and he is good to me. We've reached 50 years married and I think that is because we have patience. It's important to have a lot of patience in marriage. But mainly love. After some years it changes to a friendlier love - the same strength but with a different face.

My husband eats everything but is very particular about the quality of his food. He loves my classic Sicilian *sugo*. First I cook big pieces of veal. After it's cooked I add pork, chopped up sausages and meatballs. It cooks for at least three hours with tomato sauce. The special ingredient is my homemade *vino cotto* - cooked wine - which has a very particular, rich flavour. It's made by boiling muscat wine with grape vine ash, which is then sieved and reduced down again into a thick syrup. I learnt this from my grandmother. Four litres of red wine boils down to about one litre of *vino cotto*.

—

Nonna Dora

NONNA DORA'S AUBERGINE
SALAD (*Caponata*)

INGREDIENTS
(*Feeds 6-8*)

— 2 celery stalks, cut into
0.5cm (¼in) crescents
— 3 aubergines, peeled and
cut into 2cm (¾in) cubes
— 3 red peppers, deseeded
and cut into 2cm (¾in)
cubes
— olive oil, for frying
— ½ onion, roughly diced
— 1 tbsp capers
— 100g (½ cup) pitted green
olives, roughly chopped
— 3 basil stalks with the leaves
on, plus more to serve
— 1½ tbsp sugar
— 3 tbsp red wine vinegar
— 1 tsp salt
— toasted pine nuts, to serve

METHOD

1. Put a pan of water on to boil and blanch the celery for 3–4 minutes to soften.
   Drain and set aside.

2. If you have a deep fryer, set it up for the aubergines and peppers. Deep fry in
   batches until browned and sticky-looking, then set aside. Alternatively, cook
   them in batches of olive oil.

3. In a sauté pan fry the onion until starting to brown. Add the capers, olives and
   blanched celery, and fry in the oil some more.

4. Add the fried aubergine and peppers and the basil to the pan. Stir in the sugar,
   red wine vinegar and salt. Continue to cook for about 10 minutes then turn
   off the heat, put the lid on and leave for a few minutes to allow the flavours to
   meld in the residual heat.

5. Serve warm on toasted bread with pine nuts and torn basil on top.

VEGETABLES

SHEWA

Tum'tumo is best made with berbere, an intense terracotta-coloured spice blend that Ethiopian and Eritrean recipes use for big flavour. Shewa has great bags of it in the kitchen and says that if you can't find it in big supermarkets or ethnic stores, it can happily be replaced by cayenne pepper. Shewa also uses a spice blend she makes by throwing an equal measure of nigella seeds, cardamom, cloves and ajwain seeds into a coffee grinder for a quick blast.

Shewa served the *tum'tumo* with kale steamed with garlic and bay leaves, and another dish of mustard leaves and spinach boiled with bright orange squash. These sat atop the *injera*, the sour, pancake-like flatbread Eritreans use as base plate and cutlery in one.

We all ate with our fingers, gathered around one large *injera*, spooning blobs of curry onto its airy surface, tearing and gathering as much as possible in one pinch, guided by Shewa the Expert Ripper. Never has anyone made hand-eating look so elegant while moving us to tears with remarkable stories.

Born: *Ethiopia, 1958*
Mother tongue: *Tigrinya and Amharic*
Grandchildren: *Sami, Zoe, Noemi*
They call her: *Abayeye*

Food is important. It's like fuel to a car but we shouldn't be too obsessed about it. As long as you have something to eat, that's the important thing. Being from Eritrea and having lived in Ethiopia has shaped how I see food. When my boys were younger and would ask what we were having for dinner, I would say, 'We're going to eat food,' not list their choices. There are so many mothers and grandmothers who can't feed their own families in this world that we should respect food and be happy with what we have.

When I was 18 it got too unsafe for me to stay in Ethiopia, so I left to go back to Eritrea. I was the only youngster left in the city because everyone had left to join the guerrillas. We (the Eritreans) were fighting for independence from Ethiopia. All the youngsters fled to the fields to become guerrilla fighters. This was in 1978. So I had to leave. When I went back to Eritrea, the soldiers put me in prison because we were still under Ethiopian rule and they thought I was going to leave and join the other fighters.

I went to prison twice, so my family insisted I either join the Eritrean fighters or leave. I didn't want to be in this war. I wasn't up to it. I was looking forward to meeting my boyfriend (my now husband) so I thought it was better I didn't go. Instead, I walked through the desert towards Sudan.

Of course I got lost. I left Eritrea in January and I got to Sudan in August. I was by myself and had to stay with nomads in the desert. The land was completely flat and I couldn't navigate it at all. I just collected dates and fruits on the way for a little nutrition, but it was so dry and arid that barely anything grew out there.

When I arrived in Sudan, I didn't have anything. No clothes, no shoes. Nothing. The final leg of the journey was for eight days and eight nights with little food or water and I was completely alone. My (now) husband thought I didn't want to be with him because he hadn't heard from me in such a long time.

The first thing I did was find an Eritrean family and ask to have a shower. I asked for two buckets of water, a towel and some soap. I had only sipped at the little water I had left and eaten dates for eight days. I didn't even know how long it would take me to arrive, so when I did arrive, it was a great relief.

I never thought I would die though. Someone asked me, 'After all this, were you scared?' I was never scared. I always think, 'Yesterday is finished so I can now look forward to tomorrow. Tomorrow, you don't know what life is going to bring and what is going to happen to you. Whatever is going to come is going to come. You have to embrace it.'

—

Abayeye Shewa

ABAYEYE SHEWA'S ERITREAN BERBERE SPICED LENTILS (*Tum'tumo*)

INGREDIENTS
(*Feeds 4*)

— 400g (2 cups) red lentils
— 1 tbsp berbere spice mix
  (see mix below)
— 1 tbsp sunflower oil
— 2 onions (red or white),
  finely diced
— 3 garlic cloves, finely chopped
— 2 tsp sea salt

FOR THE BERBERE SPICE MIX
(*Makes about 5 tbsp*)

— 1 tbsp dried chilli
— 1 tbsp nigella seeds
— 1 tbsp cardamom,
  shells removed
— 1 tbsp cloves
— 1 tbsp cumin seeds

METHOD

1. If you have time, soak your lentils for 15–30 minutes before cooking to help with digestion. If not, simply rinse under a cold tap; they will still cook fine.

2. If you are making your own berbere blend, do this now by grinding all the listed spices together. You'll have some left to play with in the future.

3. Heat the sunflower oil in a pan and soften the onions. Add the chopped garlic and berbere, stir for 1 minute, and follow with the red lentils (drained and rinsed, if soaked).

4. Add boiling water to cover the lentils and then the same amount of water again. Simmer on a low heat for 10–15 minutes, stirring every so often to help the lentils break down and stop it sticking on the bottom of the pan.

5. When the lentils have broken down and combined, remove from the heat, season with 2 tsp of sea salt and serve.

ABAYEYE SHEWA'S SPICED SQUASH AND SPINACH STEW

INGREDIENTS
(*Feeds 4*)

— 500g (1lb) crown prince
  squash, butternut squash
  or another hard-skinned
  squash, peeled, seeded
  and cut into 2cm (¾in) cubes
— 3 tbsp sunflower oil
— 2 onions, finely chopped
— 2 garlic cloves, finely chopped
— 1 tbsp berbere spice mix
— 3 bunches mature
  spinach, washed and
  roughly chopped

METHOD

1. Prepare the squash and set aside.

2. Heat the oil and soften the onion in a large pan and then stir in the garlic and berbere for 2 minutes.

3. Add the spinach with 1cm (½in) boiling water. Place the lid on to steam until just wilted.

4. Next add the squash pieces and pour over another 100ml (scant ½ cup) boiling water. Stir the spinach and squash together. Partly cover the pan and simmer for 20 minutes, or until the squash is tender.

Tip: You can use bags of baby spinach for this (around 300g/10 cups) but add them in 5 minutes before the end to wilt instead - the tender leaves will more easily overcook.

ABAYEYE SHEWA'S KALE AND MUSTARD LEAVES COOKED WITH GARLIC

INGREDIENTS
(Feeds 4)

— 2 tbsp olive oil
— 3 garlic cloves, finely chopped
— 1 tsp ground rosemary or a bay leaf
— 600g (1¼lb) kale, stems removed and very finely chopped (or half kale and half green mustard leaves)
— 1 long red pepper, finely diced (Shewa likes to add this for colour)

METHOD

1. Heat 1 tbsp oil in a large saucepan, and add the garlic and rosemary or bay leaf. Stir for a couple of minutes until the aromas are released.

2. Make sure your kale and mustard leaves (if using) are really finely chopped: this will give a better texture when cooked. Rinse and put in the saucepan without drying, stirring to coat in the garlic and herbs. Add 0.5cm (¼in) of boiling water to the pan, put a lid on and steam the greens for 10–15 minutes – they are supposed to be quite cooked down.

3. Once the greens are soft and wilted, stir in the red pepper. Season to taste and toss with 1 tbsp olive oil before transferring to a serving dish.

Grandmother Narmada Lakhani's Gujarati Corn on the Cob Curry

Meera Sodha, food writer

Ingredients

- 120g (1 cup) unsalted peanuts, preferably red-skinned (plus extra to serve)
- 6 corncobs
- 5 tbsp rapeseed oil
- 60g (⅔ cup) chickpea (gram) flour
- 300ml (1¼ cups) Greek yoghurt
- 1½ tsp salt
- ½ tsp ground turmeric
- 1½ tsp chilli powder
- 1 tsp caster sugar

At the age of 83 my grandma has somewhat unreliable hips, but I have never seen her move so quickly to the dining table as when this curry is on the menu. It's not just one of her favourites, it's also on the A-list of curries for a lot of Gujaratis. There are no onions or garlic in this dish, but the ground peanuts, chickpea flour and yoghurt add a real depth of flavour and savoury nuttiness.

Feeds 8-10

1. Grind the peanuts to a fine consistency in a spice grinder or food processor and set aside.

2. Dehusk the cobs and pull off any silky strands.

3. Make a deep horizontal cut halfway down each cob and break in half.

4. Bring a pan of water to the boil, add the corn and boil for 6–8 minutes, until tender, then drain.

5. Put the oil into a large, lidded frying pan over a low–medium heat and, once hot, add the chickpea flour, stirring continuously to smooth out any lumps. After around 4 minutes it will start to turn a pinkish brown. When it does, add the ground peanuts, turn the heat right down and cook for 5 minutes, stirring frequently.

6. Add the yoghurt, salt, turmeric, chilli powder and sugar to the pan. Stir to mix, then increase the heat to medium. Slowly ladle in 600ml (2½ cups) of water, stirring until you have a smooth consistency.

7. Put the corncobs into the pan, cover with the lid and leave to heat through for around 5 minutes, until the sauce is the consistency of double cream. Transfer to a serving dish or individual bowls and scatter over some crushed peanuts. Serve with rice or chapatis and encourage people to get stuck in with their hands.

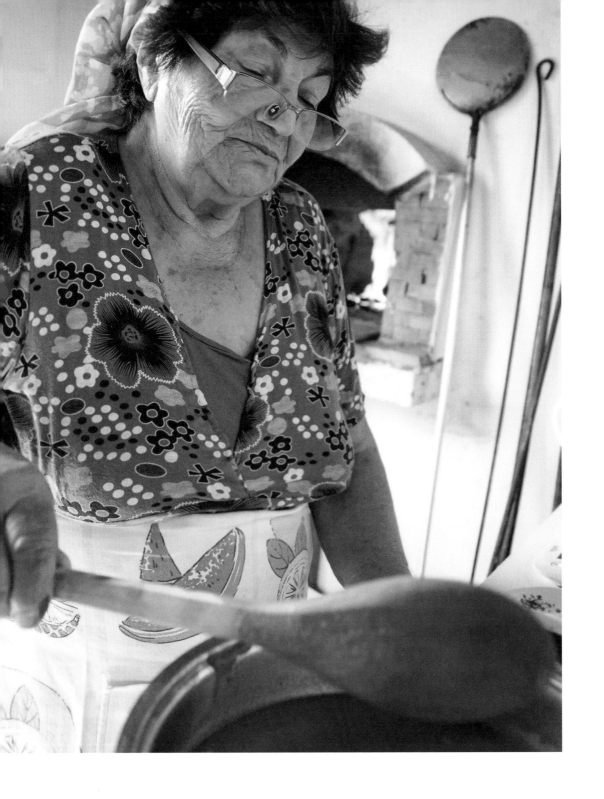

CICCINA

In the south of Sicily in the countryside of Licata, we spent a day learning to roll fresh pasta with Nonna Ciccina in her outdoor kitchen. Cooking up a *taiano* is a real process, usually reserved for feasting days like New Year's or Ferragosto (the very special saint's day of 15 August).

First Ciccina prepared the pasta dough, returning to knead and roll hundreds of intricate individual pieces of *strozzapreti* (you can, of course, just use a good-quality shop-/deli-bought pasta), before moving on to the many individual components that make up the layers of a traditional Sicilian *pasta al forno* (oven-baked pasta).

After five hours of preparation, countless stages and continual poking of the traditional wood-fired oven from an impatient Ciccina, the *taiano* was ready. What we were not counting on was the entire tray being dropped on the floor by her son-in-law before it even reached the table. We saw the funny side, but tensions in the family were at an all-time high. She was not a happy Nonna.

Thankfully, our photographer, Ella, is vegetarian and we'd made a spare veggie tray for her, so no harm done.

Born: *Licata, Sicily, 1936*
Mother tongue: *Italian*
Grandchild: *Alessandra*
She calls her: *Nonna*

When I was younger, we had no such thing as this *primi*, *secondi* nonsense. We just put everything we had on the table and we'd feast on special occasions. *Taiano* is one of my favourite dishes and I love it because I make it with all my heart, because it's for special occasions. We would prepare this three or four days in advance of the big occasion because it's such a lengthy process. Traditionally, we would make this specifically for New Year here in Sicily. Now when the family comes together, I'll also make it on a Sunday.

I began to roll pasta from when I was very young, probably from the age of 10. In fact, I still roll my pasta on the same wooden board I learned on. I like making the pasta myself; it reminds me of the times spent with my own mother and grandmother, rolling pasta together.

Around that time, Sicily was being heavily bombarded. I remember because we would hide out in the countryside during the bombardments. Of course, the reason for leaving our home in town was the war, but I loved it because it meant I could be in the countryside. We had a wooden cart that was pulled by donkeys and we'd travel from town in it.

We grew our own wheat on a plot of land and we'd make our own flour. Depending on the season, I'd plant broccoli, potatoes, onions, work on the cotton harvest or the grape harvest, then of course we'd make wine. The land was basically our livelihood.

I was 26 years old when I married, which was quite late for those days. He was my first and only love and a golden man. He left for 14 years to work in Germany and I never went to visit him once. He'd come twice a year and they were really the only times we would go out. I didn't dare go out without him.

I would ask him what he was up to over there and he'd always respond, 'I am faithful to you,' but you never really know. He was a man. I don't know what exactly he was doing for those years, but what I do know was that he was coming back to me.

I don't like the life young people lead these days. For us, it was one man for ever. Don't imagine that when you're married to someone, there won't be fights and that everything will be perfect. After 10 years of marriage now, people can divorce and exchange partners. Do you think that's a better life than the one I led? The most important thing is respect and understanding between a couple. You have to love them and respect them, in spite of it all.
—

Nonna Ciccina

NONNA CICCINA'S SICILIAN VEGETARIAN PASTA BAKE (*Taiano*)

INGREDIENTS
(Feeds 4)

— 5 tbsp olive oil
— 1 small onion, finely diced
— 1 small carrot, finely diced
— 100g (⅔ cup) peas, fresh or frozen (optional)
— 700g (3 cups) passata
— bunch fresh basil, leaves picked
— 500g (3¾ cups) cauliflower, cut into small florets and boiled with a pinch of salt until soft
— 400g (14oz) *strozzapreti* pasta (or another good-quality dried pasta)
— 125g (½ cup) ricotta
— 3 eggs: 2 hard-boiled and 1 whisked to pour over before cooking
— 50g (1¾oz) parmesan

METHOD

1. For the *sugo* (tomato sauce): heat a glug of olive oil in a large lidded pan and fry half the chopped onion and half the carrot until soft and golden. Stir in the peas a couple of pinches of salt for 1 minute.

2. Add the passata, then fill the empty containers with water and add this to the pan as well. Add a good grind of salt and black pepper, and a pinch of sugar to reduce the acidity of the tomatoes.

3. Add the basil leaves, leaving a few to garnish. Bring to the boil then turn down to a simmer with the lid on. Allow to simmer for 1 hour while you prepare the other layers of the dish.

4. For the cauliflower: heat a glug of olive oil in another pan and fry the other half of the onion and carrot until soft. Add your pre-boiled cauliflower florets, drizzle in more olive oil and cook on a low heat for 3–4 minutes until it has soaked up the oil. Take off the heat, season and set aside.

5. For the pasta: boil water for your pasta and add salt (Ciccina says don't add oil!). Wait until it's bubbling away before you add the pasta and cook 2 minutes less than the time indicated on the packet to ensure it's al dente. Drain the pasta, keeping a ladleful of cooking water to help your pasta bind with the *sugo* better.

6. Preheat oven to 200°C/180°C fan/400°F/gas 6.

7. Now for the layering: drizzle a 20 x 30cm (8 x 12in) tray with olive oil followed by a layer of pasta and a ladle of *sugo* to cover, then crumbled fresh ricotta, crumbled cauliflower florets and sliced boiled egg.

8. Then repeat, until your tray is full. Finish with a hefty grating of parmesan, black pepper, a drizzle of olive oil and the whisked egg poured over your tray of ingredients before it goes in the oven for 30 minutes. When it's caramelised on top, remove from the oven carefully and serve with more parmesan, the reserved basil leaves and a good Italian vino.

RAJNI

Having launched this project with our own two grandmothers, Rajni was our first 'unknown' and thus most nerve-wracking. We didn't yet have our 'routine' nailed, and we'd driven all the way to an unknown street in Leicester, trusting her granddaughter Ria's insistence that Rajni was a culinary legend. Ria was not biased; the nerves evaporated and it was one of our favourite days. We went straight into the kitchen, already full of flavour, and watched her casually make three curries, lassis and dessert in a sort of narrated performance, wearing a beautiful turmeric-coloured sari.

These photos by Ella are still some of our absolute favourites. At one point we had Rajni down on her knees with the incredible spread laid out on the floor, all elegant hands and heavy gold bangle, pretending to serve her curries. She was incredibly game and patient. Finally we all sat down: the three of us, her sister, daughter and granddaughter (husband banished to the study for the duration). We sat around the table for about two hours, sharing food and stories.

To this day, in any yoghurt-based scenario we still quote Rajni, who was absolutely insistent that yoghurt is the secret to eternal youth.

Born: *Tanzania, 1939*
Mother tongue: *Kutchi*
Grandchildren: *Ria, Sonia, Dhruti, Jay*
They call her: *Dadi*

If I don't like someone's food, I won't eat it. The day before yesterday, my friend told me, 'My curry is the best.' I said, 'NO! My curry is best, I don't want to eat your curry.' We all make the same curry differently. We each have our own way.

I keep my mothers alive in my food. My Gujarati mother made savouries like no one else and my mother-in-law taught me how to make sweet dishes. We show love for our children by cooking. Before the grandchildren visit, I ask them, 'What can I make for you? What do you want to take home with you? You call me in time and I make it for you to take back.' I always have savoury snacks ready in the cupboard for them.

I'd die without my tomato purée. My skin isn't so wrinkly and I swear to everybody it's the yoghurt. Yoghurt, yoghurt, yoghurt! I've never eaten meat or eggs. Growing up, we always ate Indian food – mainly vegetables – even when I lived in Tanzania. I struggled in the 70s when I moved to England. It wasn't easy to get hold of the ingredients here, but I had to adjust.

You have to compromise with your life. I met my husband six months after we were married. I agreed with my father that I would marry him and we had separate ceremonies, me in India, him in Tanzania. I remember, I was so skinny – only 75lbs – because I had nearly died of typhoid before the wedding. I saw him for the first time after it was all decided that we would be together for life. To me, it wasn't a choice or option to think it wouldn't work. In our time, we wouldn't even consider that we weren't happy or it didn't work. It just did work.

I'm always happy. Telling people your problems only creates more problems for you. I never complain. Well, sometimes I ask my husband, 'Why don't you buy me sari?' He says, 'Buy it yourself.' We argue and sometimes he gives up, other times I give up, but for a happy marriage for 56 years, we compromised. If life goes quiet, I tell him, 'We haven't argued for a long time. I don't like it! It's so quiet and silent.'

I can't stand silence. When I came to England I cried because of it – especially on Sundays, because everything was closed. I like to be around people. I was so used to that in Tanzania. I missed my family and I couldn't get anything I wanted for my cooking. I lost weight. I couldn't eat. The weather was so cold but I wanted to go out in just my sari. I had to wear shoes and trousers and tops and a heavy coat. This was all new to me. My family were rich and we had servants where we lived in Tanzania. Here, I learned to work hard for everything we have.

The most important thing I have learned in life is economise. I learned this from my husband. He's still working and he's 82. I make my own saris and sell them, then I give the money I make to charity. That is what you must do to stay young – just keep going, keep doing.

—

Dadi Rajni

DADI RAJNI'S GUJARATI DRY VEGETABLE CURRY (*Sambhariya*)

INGREDIENTS

(Feeds 8 as part of a thali or 4 as a main)

— 500g (1lb) new potatoes
— 8 tbsp sunflower oil
— 2 aubergines, cut into large chunks
— 2 green peppers, roughly cut into 3cm (1¼in) squares
— 450–500g (1lb) small red onions, peeled, with a cross shape cut to the centre

FOR THE COOKING SPICES

— 2 green bird's-eye chillies, whole with a small slit made in the side
— 2 tsp mustard seeds
— 1 tsp fenugreek seeds
— ½ tsp asafoetida
— 5 dried curry leaves

FOR THE MASALA

— 80g (scant 1 cup) chickpea (gram) flour
— 2 tbsp fresh coriander, stalks removed and leaves finely chopped
— 1 tbsp ground cumin
— 1 tsp turmeric
— 1 tsp chilli powder
— 2 tsp salt
— 2 tsp caster sugar

METHOD

1. Parboil the new potatoes.

2. Prepare the masala by combining all the ingredients in a mixing bowl.

3. In a frying pan heat ½ tbsp sunflower oil. Add the masala and toast the mix to bring out the flavours, stirring constantly for 5 minutes until it is more yellow in colour, then take off the heat.

4. Put 4 tbsp sunflower oil into a large pan on a medium–low heat. Add the drained potatoes and put the lid on and cook for 8–10 minutes, or until they have started to soften and turn golden in places. Shake the pan so the potatoes get heat on all sides.

5. Put the cut-up aubergines and peppers into a bowl. Stuff some of the masala into each of the onions, pulling apart the cut to stuff as much as you can (about half the mix). Do this over the bowl of vegetables so no masala is wasted.

6. Next, turn the heat down on the potato pan while you add all the cooking spices. Heat for 2 minutes until they crackle and release their scent.

7. Now add the stuffed onions, aubergines and peppers. Sprinkle over 2 tbsp masala mix and 2 more tbsp oil. Stir gently to coat and put the lid on again. Cook on low heat until the veg is nearly soft (around 25 minutes). Keep an eye on it in case it starts sticking (it always does a bit, says Rajni). If it's sticking, turn the heat lower, add a little more oil and a splash of water if necessary.

8. When the veg is soft, add the remaining 2 tbsp oil and sprinkle in the rest of the masala and stir to coat. Cook for 5 minutes more for the mixture to really stick to the veg and warm through. Test the seasoning and serve with lots of yoghurt, fresh coriander and chapati as a main, or to create a proper Indian thali like Rajni you could also add a serving of raita, a simple red lentil dahl, rice and a lassi.

Babi Ivanka's Slovenian Potato Salad

Ana Kerin, founder of Kana London

Ingredients

— 3 medium, waxy potatoes
— 1 head of radicchio
   (not chicory –
   the purple kind)
— pumpkin-seed oil
— apple cider vinegar

My grandmother was a complete genius. She was an artist and her medium was food. She was constantly inventing new things. She grew up in the middle of a forest in Slovenia where bears lived, with her own grandma and seven aunts. It was a complete fairy-tale. They were constantly battling with the forest, trying to defend their little allotments and grow beans, potatoes and hemp.

She was extremely beautiful. She had long dark hair, olive skin, piercing green eyes. Despite her rural upbringing, she was always dressed immaculately. She would wear sheer knitwear with lacy bras underneath and she had perfect nails despite being out in the garden daily.

There are thousands of potato recipes in Slovenia because they were cheap and in abundance. So people would try and be creative with their recipes – my grandmother included. For a quick lunch, we often had a radicchio with potato on top, which would soften the bitterness of the radicchio.

Depending on where in Slovenia, this potato salad recipe varies greatly. Babi was from the Italian border, so she originally made this with olive oil, but when she married my grandfather from the east – where pumpkins grow in the beautiful flatlands – the olive oil was ditched for pumpkin-seed oil.

For my grandmother it was completely unacceptable to cut the potato before it was boiled. She would put the entire potato in the pan to boil, to keep the flavour. She had so much resistance to the heat that she'd peel it right away after it came out of the pan. One thing I still struggle with.

Feeds 4 as a side dish

1. Put the potatoes in a pan of cold, unsalted water. Bring to the boil and then turn to medium and cook for around 20 minutes, or until you can stick a fork into the potatoes and they are soft but not falling apart.

2. While the potatoes boil, separate all the leaves from the radicchio head. Put the leaves in a sink full of cold water.

3. Babi Ivanka would then take the leaves, place an individual leaf lengthways on a chopping board, roll it into a tube-like shape and begin to slice from one end at 0.5cm (¼in) intervals to produce very thin strips of lettuce. Do this with all of the leaves and place them at the bottom of your salad bowl.

4. Once the potatoes are ready, use your fork to hold the potato and peel the skin away with a very sharp knife and then slice into circles about 0.5cm (¼in) thick.

5. While the potatoes are still hot, place them on top of the radicchio.

6. Splash with a generous amount of pumpkin-seed oil – this is a very important part of the recipe and is not replaceable with another oil.

7. Season generously with salt, sprinkle apple cider vinegar over, mix and eat right away.

TISH

It was on the Los Angeles leg of our five-week road trip across the USA that we had perhaps the most (and only) terrifying granny experience. We had a run-in with Skid Row - an apocalyptic portion of LA - 50 blocks of homeless people living in tents, and we'd decided it was a good idea to just 'nip through'. It didn't seem so big on the map, Iska had pointed out. It was.

Ironically, two homeless grandmas, aggressively shoving shopping trolleys towards us, began to chase us down the street. 'I'm gon' get me a new bag,' they cackled. We were the only people stupid enough to have walked down there. They meant our bags.

We managed to outrun them - only just. In need of a beer, we zipped up to a hotel roof garden, where we met Alexa, who by some miracle turned our day around. Luck would have it that her mother, activist Tish, is a grandma - and a keen cook. Within a few hours, we were en route to Hollywood to rustle up an insanely colourful salad with Tish, who whisked us through her protest-reportage photography between blanching asparagus and expertly slicing at every vegetable and fruit known to man.

Born: *New York, USA, 1949*
Mother tongue: *American English*
Grandchildren: *Lindsay, Teagan, Arden, Gaspar*
They call her: *Jeune Tish*

The secret of good salad dressing is mixing. You should mix your dressing really well before it goes on, rather than dress with each individual ingredient at the end. I like to make a mix of my dressing in advance of it all going on – except the salt. I love the jammy part of this dressing at the end, when it all comes out. It's just a little treat on this very healthy dish. Then I salt at the very end because it gets lost if it goes in with the dressing.

I love farmers' markets and eating organic. It's one of the beautiful things about living in Los Angeles, this access we have to such good produce. I like to eat well and it's important to me to have

wholesome ingredients. I also use filtered water to cook with because you know water has lead and chlorine in it?

When I grew up, the big sort of appetiser of the 1950s and 60s was this grapefruit and avocado in a shrimp cocktail dish. Fruit would feature a lot in our salads and savoury dishes. My mother would throw these Jackie Kennedy-type cocktail parties with a swanky New York crowd.

My family's a little scandalous. My dad started a lingerie company that changed the American underwear industry. I grew up very snobby on Park Avenue. Went to an all-girls' school. I was a debutante

with Tricia Nixon. It was a sort of 'coming out' party where you're introduced into society. We call it a 'cotillion'. I hated it. I was very chubby and I found it extremely hard. I was so angry about being forced to do it.

And you know, when they fall, they fall hard. After that I became a renegade hippie. I worked on Broadway as an actor. I lived in London in the late 60s. It was this extraordinary era to be young. I was really in it. That's when I started photographing. I worked with David Bailey. It was the Biba era, and he photographed me.

I actually first came to California on a whim to visit a friend of mine, and she was a photographer and I had 90 rolls of film, so I came here to stay with her. This sort of hippie life appealed to me at that time. I guess it was me rebelling against everything I had been raised into.

This sort of privileged New York scene. I wanted something different for myself.

I've done all sorts. I was an actor. When I lived in London I worked in opera. I did ski photography. I started photographing in 1967 for the London *Evening Standard*. I went to the Democratic Republic of the Congo to be with rebel soldiers to take photographs of lowland gorilla, who are now unfortunately being poached. I won awards for those. I became friends with those gorillas. I had a King Kong experience. Now I'm a screenwriter too.

A big part of my life has been documenting protest and human-rights issues. I work as a documentary photographer for the United Nations, the Conflict Awareness Project and the United States Veterans Alliance. In the last few years I've been really focused on

activism that's been borne of this huge wave of unrest here in the States.

I'm doing a book of all my protest photography, charting social-change movements that have been all over the news in the past years. I've been at all of these protests, in the crowd with the people. It's so important to stand for what we believe in. The stuff going on in the country really is disgusting. I've been there at protests for the fight for women's rights and gender equality, immigration rights, civil liberties, gun violence, and the environment. The least I can do is document our resistance to all of this injustice and share that with the world through my photography. I even have a podcast. I guess I do quite a lot. I've always had a busy, chaotic and unpredictable life. That's just life.

—

Jeune Tish

JEUNE TISH'S CALIFORNIAN SUNSHINE SALAD

INGREDIENTS
(Feeds 4)

— handful hazelnuts
— bunch asparagus,
  woody ends removed
— 1 x 70g (2½oz) bag rocket
— 1 butter lettuce, torn
— ½ red pepper, sliced into
  thin pieces
— 150g (1 cup) peas (fresh or
  frozen peas cooked and
  dunked in cold water)
— 12 mixed cherry
  tomatoes, halved
— 1 avocado, peeled,
  stoned and sliced
— 4 or 5 radishes, finely sliced
— 1 grapefruit
— 1 tangerine
— handful raspberries

FOR THE CROUTONS

— 1 demi-baguette, sliced into
  1.5cm (⅔ in) rounds
— 2 garlic cloves, crushed
— 2 tbsp olive oil

FOR THE DRESSING

— 1 tsp raspberry jam
— juice of 2 limes
— 5 tbsp olive oil
— 2 tbsp balsamic vinegar
— pinch Himalayan salt

METHOD

1. Preheat oven to 180°C/160°C fan/350°F/gas 4. First, make the croutons: take your slices of baguette (if you bought a big one, cut the rounds into halves). Mix the garlic and olive oil in a bowl with a pinch of salt and brush or rub this onto the bread. Put on a tray in the oven to toast for 15–20 minutes, rotating the tray halfway through, until golden.

2. At the same time, pop the hazelnuts on a baking tray and put them in to toast for 4–5 minutes. Set a timer and make sure they don't catch.

3. Next make the dressing: in an old clean jar put all the dressing ingredients and shake to combine, then set aside.

4. Steam the asparagus in a pan with a lid and a little water for 4–5 minutes, keeping them al dente. Set aside.

5. Prepare all the veg and citrus fruit. Slice the top and bottom off the grapefruit and tangerine to start segmenting. Place the flat edge on the chopping board and cut the skin off the sides, then cut along the edge of each segment to extract them, trying to lose all the pith.

6. Find a big serving plate and start building up the salad, starting with the butter lettuce, with the asparagus around the edge pointing out like sunrays. Fill the plate with all the fruit and vegetables however you like, add the croutons and drizzle over the dressing.

Granny Kathryn's Cucumber and Tarragon Salad

Rosie Birkett, food writer and stylist

Ingredients

— 1 cucumber
— 1 tsp caster sugar
— 1 tbsp tarragon or white wine vinegar
— 80ml (5 tbsp) double cream
— 1 tsp Dijon mustard, optional
— 1½ tbsp rapeseed or vegetable oil
— ¼ tsp ground white pepper
— small bunch fresh chives, finely chopped
— few leaves of tarragon

My granny Kathryn, my dad's mum, was a serious, elegant and intelligent woman that I always remember speaking her mind. Before having children, Granny had previously worked as a governess, and she had an authority and grandness to her that never left, even when she was incredibly old, which sometimes made her rather formidable. Despite this, she had a very kind nature, and a great deal of patience, which was tested to the maximum while trying to teach me to knit.

She lost her husband Phillip, an architect, very young from bone cancer when my father was just a baby, and brought him and his two sisters up on her own through rationing. This undoubtedly instilled a thriftiness and knack for eking out food into her cooking, and I think this salad is a perfect example of this – it takes a few quite simple ingredients and combines them to make something truly delicious and special.

Granny always laid on a nice home-cooked meal, and often made this salad, laying it out on the table with some ham and perhaps some cold cuts. It's adapted from a very old Penguin cordon bleu cookbook, which, along with Elizabeth David's *Provincial French Cooking*, was her go-to cookbook, and it might just explain my lifelong love of tarragon.

Feeds 2-4 as a side

1. Peel the cucumber, slice as thinly as possible, salt it lightly and press it down between two plates with a weight on top. Leave for 30 minutes, then tip off any liquid.

2. Mix the sugar and vinegar together, stir in the cream and Dijon (if using), then add the oil by degrees, whisking until you're happy with the texture (it should be a thin salad cream you're able to drizzle; you can thin with 1 tsp of warm water if needed), then season with the white pepper.

3. Arrange the drained cucumber in a shallow dish, spoon over the dressing – just use what you need and serve the rest alongside or save for another salad – and scatter the top with chives and tarragon.

JEAN

Jean is a woman in demand. She's celebrated at the Caribbean society for her delicious Jamaican dishes and spends much of the week preparing food for different events, grandchildren and for church on Saturday. So we were lucky to get a whole afternoon of uninterrupted Jean time.

As the date approached, we rang a couple of times to check we were still ON. Which seemed to irk Jean. Why would we assume she might forget?! This is very Jean - forthright and bold, with a great wit and no time for fuss.

We squeezed into the kitchen to watch her elegant hands prepare vegetables as she spoke. We became rather taken with her electric tin opener and finding photos of the ackee fruit in its pre-canned form. Then once the food was ready, we rearranged the living room to find the best light for shooting the dish. The concept of 'food styling' is usually rather bizarre to our grannies (who just want us to 'eat before it gets cold!') but it did not rattle Jean. Far too cool and calm.

We had a long lunch together - Jean had also prepared the traditional ackee and saltfish for us to try - filled with stories of her sister and times in Jamaica. She called us 'babes' as we left the house and we responded with a loud 'bye babes!' in unison. Which made us all crack up at the relaxed conviviality of it all.

Born: *Jamaica, 1943*
Mother tongue: *English and Patwah*
Granchildren: *Sheldon, Charise, Shaunna, Sherelle, Cheniell, Yasmin, Shae, Cyon, Jade, Jentae, Jeihim, Juranuel, Neriyah*
They call her: *Nan*

This is a traditional Jamaican dish that instantly takes me back. It takes me back to that island and to the smells that hit you over the head coming from people's homes. The original is with saltfish, but I'm vegan and have been a vegetable convert for quite some time now.

The reason for this was that two years back I was diagnosed with breast cancer. Of my own accord, I decided to change the way I eat. I cut out dairy, meat and fish. The fish really was tough to resist when I went back to Jamaica last year, though. Back home, the fish we have is fresh - just come in from the sea - so it's really delicious.

Still, if I don't look after myself, no one else is going to do it for me. So I say no to fish, and lots of other things. Cancer feeds on sugar, so I've cut that out too. If the family comes over, I'll cook chicken and fish for them but I don't eat it myself. My kitchen might be small but I do manage to do a lot of cooking in spite of that.

I like to experiment with my cooking. I try my best to be healthy, and even cake that I make I come up with my own healthy recipes. I use dates and coconut oil to make sweet cakes. You have to learn to be creative when you have five children. I would never let my kids go and buy sandwiches for school. It was ackee and saltfish and fried dumplings. I would make home-made pizza too. It's so important to use ingredients in their purest form. That way we know exactly what is going into our bodies.

Church is also a big part of my life. I'm a Seventh Day Adventist, which means on Friday evening to Saturday evening, I don't do a thing (like cooking or cleaning). We believe that Jesus is the Son of God and that he is coming soon, as the King of Kings. The Bible clearly states that this will happen. My children don't believe in church, but I do tell them the Lord is coming soon. They just say, 'OK, OK, Mummy.' The grandchildren came with me until they became a bit older.

I arrived in the UK in 1962 from Jamaica because my sisters were here. They sent for me to come and painted such a picture of England. You know, there was all this talk of Buckingham Palace and so, growing up in Jamaica, you think everyone in England lives in palaces. Everybody was coming at the time. It was exciting.

I came by ship and shared a cabin with six other girls. I rather quite liked that three-week journey. I just remember arriving and thinking, Is this it? I came in April and I saw the fog and all the grey as we approached and I really wondered what I had got myself into. My sisters told me nothing about the weather. I had just been fed this fantasy about palaces.

Back in Jamaica, we were under colonial rule and so we were all very impressed by this great empire. All British people living in Jamaica had money. Most of them were diplomats and they had maids, gardeners and so on. We genuinely thought we'd come to England and have that. I could barely believe white men swept the streets when I arrived in London, because in Jamaica all the white people were so rich. We thought all English people were incredibly wealthy. It didn't matter too much though, because I was well-received and I settled into a community here. That means more than wealth to me.

—

Nan Jean

NAN JEAN'S JAMAICAN VEGAN CALLALOO AND ACKEE WITH STEAMED PUMPKIN AND ROOTS

INGREDIENTS
(Feeds 4)

— 400g (14oz) cassava, peeled
  and chopped into large
  chunks (see method)
— 500g (1lb) piece yellow
  yam, peeled and chopped
  into large chunks
— 1 sweet potato (about 400g/
  14oz), peeled and chopped
  into large chunks
— 400g (14oz) pumpkin, skin
  on and chopped into large
  chunks
— 1 tbsp olive oil
— 1 red onion, peeled
  and diced
— 1 large tomato, chopped
— 1 vegetable stock cube,
  crumbled
— ½ tsp cayenne pepper
— 1 x 540g (20oz) tin callaloo
— 1 x 540g (20oz) tin ackee

METHOD

1. Set up a large steamer pan on the hob in preparation. Peel the skin off the cassava by using a sharp knife to chop it into 15cm (6in) rounds, then take each piece and lay the flat side onto the chopping board and slice downwards along the edges to remove the skin. Once peeled, chop into large chunks.

2. Add the peeled and chopped cassava, yam and sweet potato to the steamer pan for around 20 minutes, until tender. After 5 minutes of steaming, add the pumpkin.

3. Meanwhile, heat a lidded sauté pan with the oil, add the onion and soften for 8 minutes before stirring in the tomato for a minute or two.

4. Next add the stock cube and cayenne pepper, stir, and add the callaloo; cook for 5 minutes with the lid on.

5. Next add the ackee. Jean carefully stirs hers with a fork rather than a spoon from now on, so as not to break up the ackee. Cover and let it simmer for 5–10 minutes.

6. Check the steamed vegetables and if a knife goes through them easily, stop cooking – you don't want them to disintegrate.

7. When everything is done, serve the steamed vegetables with the ackee and callaloo.

Tip: You can use finely chopped fresh spinach or tender spring greens as a substitute for callaloo, or for a non-vegan version swap it for saltfish.

Jean also added 1 tbsp of annatto paste (spooned from a mysterious unlabelled jar in her fridge) for colour and for its many health benefits. Annatto (also called achiote) is a seed that grows in Jamaica and can be found as a powder or paste. Add if you can track it down!

FISH

CHULA

We were connected with Chula - full name Chulalaxana Varanand Chudadhuj - through a very helpful and witty man at the Anglo-Thai Society, who, upon proposing Chula, offered, 'If not right, I can try and seek out another innocent potential victim.'

She was more than right: exquisitely presented and very good fun. As soon as our coats were removed we were offered a glass of Moët, which we just managed to delay until the cooking was finished. Luckily that was not long, because this curry is incredibly speedy to make. With the ingredients ready laid out, it took under 15 minutes.

The house was full of colour, with Chula's oil paintings all over the walls, her 1990s stereo in the corner and accompanying pile of 'sentimental love' CDs just beside it. There were hanging glass flower lampshades, coloured candles, decorative crockery and wall-mounted plates that she'd découpaged herself.

The interview evolved and deepened as the champagne flowed. She was incredibly open and generous, with her advice, her fears and her food. Once done with mains, she disappeared with the plates and returned with a warm bowl of chopped banana blasted in the microwave with coconut milk - aka a hug in a bowl. We departed with bubbles, panang and newfound wisdom running through our veins.

Born: *Bangkok, Thailand, 1950*
Mother tongue: *Thai*
Grandchildren: *Arabella, Mimi, Dolce, Murphy*
They call her: *Grandma*

I taught myself to cook when I was living in Hong Kong and working as a flight attendant. I was just 25 and we had to cook for ourselves in our free apartment. I would ask Chinese people on the roadside to show me how to cook fried rice in the Chinese way.

At the time I was working as a flight attendant for Cathay Pacific. There were only 25 Cathay Pacific Thai girls. There were more than 1,200 applicants and I was one of the 25. I was so proud of myself. Of course I had a lot of make-up on, but I was a model at the time. I think I got the job because of my smile - I gave big smiles to everyone because I didn't know what else to do.

I was so happy and I came back home to tell my mother and my father I got the job, but they

weren't happy. They said, 'What's wrong with you? You have four maids at home! You don't have to do anything at all.'

I told them about all the other applicants and how I'd beaten them, that the Cathay airline uniform was designed by Pierre Balmain and that I wanted to travel. They didn't want me to be serving people. I got accepted for three airlines but Cathay was three times the pay. We would have breakfast in Hong Kong, lunch in Singapore, dinner in Jakarta, Indonesia overnight, then Sydney for two days and then come back. The first time I did this I slept for a full 24 hours after.

Contrary to my parents' beliefs, flying was so glamorous back then. Everyone was smoking on the plane (now I think that's disgusting). I had a cigarette holder. Can you imagine? Mostly we served steak. Lavish dinners. Everything was ready prepared. I just had to warm it in the galley.

I don't get stressed when I'm cooking for lots of people: I'm happy. Being a good hostess comes from inside of you; you have to love cooking and want to share your made-up recipes. That's why I host young Thai students who are at boarding school here in the UK. I'm the second guardian for the Thai Embassy and so, once a month, these children - sometimes up to six - come to stay with me for the weekend. I cook them Thai food. The first student I had was eight years old and he's just sent me a business-class ticket to come to his wedding. It's like being a grandmother a second time around to so many children.

Six years ago I got breast cancer. I had a mastectomy and changed my diet to be more healthy and I began making up my own recipes. I use brown rice or, if it has to be white, then I use basmati, because it grows with minerals. If I make pad thai I never add sugar and I slice carrots to use instead of the noodles. Sometimes I slice raw papaya instead of noodles.

People love it. Most people in Bangkok eat beef and pork panang but I prefer fish. That's why I am making you salmon panang. I tested all different kinds of fish, like plaice and halibut for this recipe, but salmon is the best.

When the cancer came, I thought I was going to die. I had six rounds of chemo. The third and fourth were horrible and I couldn't eat anything at all. It took me half an hour to eat one teaspoon of plain rice. Even water was very bitter tasting. Then one of my doctors said, 'OK, Chula, if you cannot drink water you must have ice cream.' I swear I survived on chocolate ice cream and pineapple juice.

I'm healthy now and I think, 'Ju st be nice to people because you don't know when you're going to die. Try and do something to make people happy.' It's why I make my healthy Thai recipes - I have about 20 and I share them with people who come to my home.

—

Grandma Chula

GRANDMA CHULA'S THAI SALMON PANANG CURRY

INGREDIENTS
(Feeds 4)

— 1 tbsp coconut oil
— 2 tbsp panang curry paste
(found in Thai supermarkets)
— 4 skinless salmon fillets
— 1 x 400ml (14oz) tin coconut
milk
— 1 tbsp coconut palm sugar
— 2 tbsp fish sauce
— handful fresh Thai basil,
leaves picked
— 2 red chillies, sliced into
thin slivers

METHOD

1. Put a frying pan large enough to hold your 4 salmon fillets on to a medium heat and add the oil.

2. Add the paste and stir (if you like your curries a little hotter, add a touch more paste).

3. Put the salmon fillets into the pan and cook for a few minutes on each side.

4. Add half the tin of coconut milk, the coconut sugar and fish sauce. Stir until the paste is fully integrated and the sauce is smooth and well combined. Careful not to break up the fillets.

5. Allow to reduce for 5 minutes and add the rest of the coconut milk and a few basil leaves and cook for a further 5 minutes.

6. When the sauce has thickened, check for seasoning and carefully transfer the curry to a serving dish. Top with a garnish of sliced chillies and basil leaves and serve with basmati rice.

Grandmother Bamrungchit Raviwongse's Thai Shrimp Paste Rice

John Chantarasak, chef

Ingredients

— 1 garlic clove
— 1 tbsp coriander root, scraped, cleaned and chopped (or finely chopped coriander stalks)
— pinch salt
— 2 tbsp vegetable oil
— 2 tbsp shrimp paste
— 2 tbsp coconut palm sugar
— 400g (3 cups) cooked jasmine rice, cooled to room temperature
— 1 large egg, whisked in a bowl with a pinch of salt

Garnishes

— 1 lime, cut into wedges
— 50g (1¾oz) dried prawns, fried until crispy
— 50g (1¾oz) Chinese sausage (*lap cheong*), sliced into 3mm (⅛in) pieces
— 100g (3½oz) green mango, shredded
— 4 Thai shallots, or 2 small round shallots, coarsely sliced
— 2 lemongrass stalks, peeled and thinly sliced
— 3 tbsp green beans, cut into 1cm (½in) pieces
— 2 tbsp fresh coriander, leaves and stem chopped
— 2 bird's-eye chillies, finely sliced
— 1 salted duck egg, cooked for 12 minutes, shelled and quartered
— raw cucumber and Chinese cabbage

My grandmother, Bamrungchit Raviwongse, on my Thai father's side of the family, still resides in Bangkok in the house my father grew up in with his two sisters. She's very old now and struggles with the day-to-day, but I still have very fond memories of my grandmother's food from our visits to Bangkok as children growing up.

My grandmother is a proud woman, known for the quality of her recipes and cooking within the family, and some of my earliest food memories are sitting around the kitchen table in Bangkok with my grandmother feeding me wonderful exotic bites from the Thai larder.

This is a family favourite dish, with rice and shrimp paste (*gapi*) at its core, two ingredients that embody the very soul of Thai cookery. It's worth sourcing good-quality Thai shrimp paste for this dish to give the depth, richness and sweetness needed for the best eating experience. Serve a mound of rice to each person with a selection of the garnishes arranged around the rice, some fresh vegetables to accompany and perhaps have a ramekin of Thai bird's-eye chillies on hand for those who love the Thai spice level.

Feeds 4

1. With a pestle and mortar, pound the garlic, coriander root (or stalks) and salt into a smooth paste.

2. In a pan or wok, fry the paste in the vegetable oil until fragrant but not coloured, then add the shrimp paste and palm sugar.

3. Simmer over a low heat until aromatic and a thick paste is achieved, around 2 minutes.

4. Add the rice to the pan and stir fry gently with the shrimp paste so the rice is easily coated but the rice remains whole. Try not to let too much of the rice catch as it fries. Taste the rice; it should be rich and pungent, well seasoned but not too salty. Add more sugar if it's too salty.

5. Cover and allow to rest for 20 minutes for the flavours to develop.

6. Smear a shallow non-stick pan with oil and pour in the whisked egg mix. Cook gently, not letting it colour; it should be the thickness of a pancake.

7. When set, remove the pan, allow it to cool slightly then roll into a cigar and slice into ribbons.

8. To serve, divide the rice onto individual plates and add a small pile of each garnish around each mound of rice.

9. To eat, squeeze over the lime wedge and mix the garnishes into the rice. Eat with the raw vegetable accompaniments and more fresh coriander.

ANASTASIA

Yiayia is an original legend: fire master and cucumber whisperer with the strongest calves in Perivoli village. Now she's a local celebrity after her film got 4.7 stars on film platform, Nowness.

We've been to Corfu a few times now, to film, cook and photograph Yiayia (a diva attitude is starting to show). The minute we get into her village, family members start appearing, from behind bougainvillea bushes, through beaded curtains, rising from their plastic chairs - approaching our Anastasia and embracing her. The biggest hug comes from Yiayia Anastasia, cheekbones smashing from the force of the two kisses. Hugs turn to abuse quite quickly. Last time she told Ana to tell me that my bum was much bigger than the previous year and then broke into hysterical laughter as this information was translated.

It's better for everyone that she keeps her manipulations to the fish, which she prepares with great prowess, then slips them into the fire at exactly the right moment, flicking olive oil across their bodies with her stick of dried oregano. Alongside Greek salad made with her own tomatoes and cucumbers, chips cooked in her own cloudy olive oil (when else do you get such luxury?), fresh lemon juice and a blob of *skordalia*, it really is Yiayia on a plate. We've styled, photographed and filmed this dish so much it's become almost iconic.

Don't be tempted to put the potatoes for *skordalia* into a blender. It will resemble wallpaper glue and cling to the roof of your mouth. We made this mistake when cooking a Yiayia-inspired supper for 40, and Yiayia was both cross and disappointed when she heard.

Born: *Corfu, Greece, 1937*
Mother tongue: *Greek*
Grandchildren: *Ippokratis, Ellie, Anastasia, George, Anastasia, Grigoris*
They call her: *Yiayia*

We eat the best food here and that's why we're all still fighting fit. It's why I'm still on my knees picking olives every November. The fish here is the best, fresh from the sea. It's caught in the morning then it's on my plate by the afternoon. That's real food that will keep you alive for years.

I've been cooking this dish for so long. We used to joke that *skordalia* isn't for a young girl that wants to be kissed. My husband, George, loved it. He would want fish every mealtime, so I learned to cook it as soon as we married. Back then, we didn't just stick it in the oven. I learned to cook on an open flame and I still only cook this way.

My mother never taught me how to do any of this - it was more about putting me to work out in the fields. I had nine other siblings and we couldn't all go to school so I never learned to read or write. Cooking and looking after my family is what I learned to do best.

I've always been poor but I've never gone hungry. When we were young we had chickens and we'd sell the eggs to make a tiny bit of money to be able to buy fish or cheese. We've always had food because we grow it. As I get older, it gets harder to do, but I still walk to my allotment for an hour every morning to harvest fresh vegetables. My oil isn't the same as the oil you

buy from any supermarket. Nothing tastes as good as the olive oil from your own olive trees.

I met my husband on the day he came to my house to ask permission to marry me. He used to pass with a horse and cart through my village. He worked as a delivery man, delivering all sorts from olives to flour, and he'd see me out in the field, working. He said he'd watched me for months before proposing. It was news to me.

He was a good-looking man and I was old by that point, 27, so I said yes. We were married eight days later. It was rushed because he'd planned to go to Germany to find

work, and I was the last thing he had to take care of before he left. I stayed for another nine months after he left and then I went to join him out there.

I was scared to go at first; I was frightened of the Germans by that point. You won't ever know what we saw in that war with the Nazis. We used to have to run and hide in ditches when aeroplanes passed over our heads. We got on well with the Italians that occupied, but it was the Germans we didn't see eye to eye with. We kept finding bodies around the island. My older brother found his friend dead. The Germans had taken his eyes out for fun. Two men from my village were

killed for going against the occupation. They were only in their teens and wanted their village back.

Germany wasn't all bad in the end, though the food was very bland and the ingredients were nothing like what I can grow myself. I gave birth to my first daughter there, but I was glad to be home a couple of years later. I haven't left this house for more than a week at a time since. George and I built this little house together and I will stay in it until the day I die.

—

Yiayia Anastasia

YIAYIA ANASTASIA'S GREEK MARINATED SEA BREAM, GREEK SALAD AND GARLIC DIP (*Skordalia*)

FOR THE SEA BREAM
(*Feeds 4-6*)

— 4 medium whole sea bream, gutted and descaled
— 1 tbsp sea salt flakes
— 2 tbsp dried oregano
— 15 tbsp olive oil
— 6 garlic cloves, finely chopped
— juice of 1 lemon

FOR THE GARLIC DIP

— 8 medium floury potatoes, peeled and halved
— 1 whole bulb garlic, cloves separated and peeled
— 100ml (7 tbsp) olive oil
— juice of 2 lemons

FOR THE GREEK SALAD

— 1 cucumber, roughly chopped
— 3 large ripe tomatoes, roughly chopped
— ½ red onion, finely sliced into half-moons
— 25 Kalamata olives
— 1 long green pepper, sliced into rings (optional)
— 1 x 200g (7oz) block feta cheese
— ½ tsp dried oregano
— 6 tbsp extra virgin olive oil
— 2 tbsp red wine vinegar

SEA BREAM

1. With a sharp knife make 3 or 4 incisions along each side of the fish and rub all over with sea salt flakes before placing in a large dish.

2. In a bowl, prepare the marinade by combining the oregano, olive oil and garlic.

3. Spoon the marinade over the fish, rubbing the mix all over and inside the fish to coat.

4. Cook the fish over a fire, on a barbecue or under a hot grill for about 8–10 minutes on each side, until the skin is blistered and the fish cooked through.

5. Squeeze the lemon juice over just before you serve (don't add during the cooking, as it makes the fish stick to the grill).

GARLIC DIP

1. Boil the potatoes in a large pan of salted water for 15–20 minutes, or until tender. Drain and leave to steam in the pan for a moment.

2. Bash the garlic cloves in a pestle and mortar until they form a paste, or finely grate. Yiayia's pestle and mortar is a thing of wonder and big enough for her to add the potatoes, but if yours isn't, simply transfer the garlic into the potato pan with the olive oil and mash or blend with a hand blender until smooth.

3. Finally, add the lemon juice and season to taste. Then add a little bit of water at a time until it reaches a runny consistency. Serve with an extra trickle of oil on top, if you like.

GREEK SALAD

1. Place the chopped cucumber, tomato and red onion into a bowl, add the Kalamata olives and mix together.

2. Spread out onto a serving dish and top with the slices of green pepper, if using, followed by a huge slab of feta and a sprinkling of oregano.

3. Layer on lashings of olive oil and a sprinkling of vinegar. Put it straight on the table and let everyone break off hunks of cheese as they serve themselves.

VERA

It may be hard to believe, but language barriers have never really been a problem for us in the collating of dishes for this book. On arrival into Moscow, we were armed only with Google Translate to make conversation with friendly taxi drivers (the first one offered us almonds on the way to the hotel and another gave us a tour of central Moscow, interjecting with little-known facts about the buildings we whizzed by). En route to Vera Petrovna, the bus driver even stopped the bus, came to our seat at the back and double checked on our map that she was taking us to the right place.

While we might have been daunted at what might as well have been hieroglyphics on the Russian underground metro network and intimidated by the language that is so far from our own, entering Vera Petrovna's was akin to walking into our own grandmothers' homes.

We don't speak a word of Russian. She knew only 'Thank you' in English. Yet somehow, the conversation flowed for an entire afternoon. This was in no small part down to grandson Denis and his girlfriend Nika, who between the flurry of activity in the kitchen, interjected in English with precise quantities for ingredients as well as detailed reminiscences that flowed out of Vera Petrovna on the subject of the good old days of the USSR.

Born: *Kazakhstan, 1946*
Mother tongue: *Russian*
Grandchild: *Denis*
He calls her: *Babushka*

I was born in Kazakhstan and when you're from my home country, you never make just one thing for your dinner guests. We fill the table. So I'm sorry, but I can't stick to one dish ever, which is why I have put on a bit of a spread for you. I always want to fill my guests. Especially if it is my grandson.

I used to cook a lot when I lived in Kazakhstan. We had a huge family. I was one of five siblings and we would always cook for our parents. Every day each of us took it in turn to cook for the rest of the family. The fish and rice dish I learned to make when I moved to Moscow, though.

In the early 1990s the Soviet Union collapsed and in those years my grandson Denis was born. I would come to Moscow from time to time to visit him but I didn't move here until 2006, much later on in my life. So we really never stop learning. It's important to keep challenging ourselves and experiencing new things. Especially as the years go by.

My mother was an excellent cook, but there are some skills you continue to improve on throughout your life. One of these is baking. I have been honing my baking skills my entire life and I still don't feel like I know all that there is to know. My bird cherry cake recipe has been of my own invention and I am very proud of it because everyone thinks it is chocolate but in reality, it isn't. It's bird cherry powder.

When I was younger, we wouldn't know where our next meal was coming from. It was hard in those days because we were part of the former Soviet Union. We would need our own animals - like cows or chickens - in order to know that we would have enough food to survive. The environment there isn't exactly the easiest one in which to grow and harvest vegetables. In winter in Siberia the mercury drops to -40°C (-40°F) sometimes. Then in summer it can hit 40°C (104°F). Also, our politics and economy were less than ideal. There just wasn't very much to go around so we made use of our land and we grew whatever we could, when we could, then we would ferment vegetables for the harsh winters.

Nowadays, children are not required to work, but back then we were forced to help our parents. They worked and it was a child's duty to provide and actually put the food on the table. We would tend the vegetables, milk the cow, cook the food. It was quite the opposite of today. We would all be responsible for something and contribute in our own way. Everyone had their own responsibility, regardless of their age. We all worked for the common good, the party.

It wasn't bad though. In the communist society we were in, when you had a big family, you were entitled to a worker. We had a housekeeper who would come and do things we children weren't able to. It was a much more interesting time to live in, before the Soviet Union broke down. Obviously I was younger, so that makes everything seem much rosier, but everyone was forced to contribute and have a job. Now there are a lot of people that don't know what to do with themselves and this situation would just not have been an issue then, because everyone had a role in society and everyone, in turn, felt useful.

At the time, we didn't know what life would be like. We didn't see beyond the Soviet Union. It was such an insular life we had, but everything was simpler and happier because we didn't have anything to compare our lives to. We might all have been poor, but everyone was in the same boat.
—

Babushka Vera

BABUSHKA VERA'S RUSSIAN RICE-STUFFED MUSTARD SALMON

INGREDIENTS
(Feeds 6–8)

— 1 whole salmon, scaled
   and gutted
— 2 tbsp smooth Russian
   mustard (or Dijon)
— 3 tbsp olive oil
— 1 tsp sea salt
— 1 tsp cracked black pepper
— 500g (2½ cups) basmati rice
— 1 onion, finely diced
— 1 carrot, grated
— 1 lemon, sliced into
   half-moons
— handful fresh dill, chopped

METHOD

1. First marinate the salmon. Lay the salmon on a good length of kitchen foil (enough to wrap it in) and prepare the marinade by mixing the mustard and 2 tbsp of the olive oil together with sea salt and freshly ground black pepper. Rub all over the salmon, wrap up and leave in the fridge overnight to soak up the flavours.

2. Preheat oven to 200°C/180°C fan/400°F/gas 6. In a saucepan, cook the rice according to pack instructions. Meanwhile, take a frying pan and soften the diced onion in the remaining 1 tbsp oil until golden at the edges, about 8 minutes. Add the carrot for the last minute or two.

3. Once the rice is done and the veg is soft, mix them together and season.

4. Retrieve your salmon from the fridge, unwrap and put it on a large baking tray (you may have to do this diagonally to make it fit; that's OK). Stuff the rice mixture inside the cavity, keeping any extra for serving. Roast in the oven for 45 minutes, until cooked through.

5. Remove the salmon from the oven and allow to rest for a few minutes before moving to a serving dish on which you've spread the remaining rice. Squeeze a little lemon on top and arrange the other slices around the dish. Sprinkle with dill and dig in.

BABUSHKA VERA'S RUSSIAN BEETROOT AND HERRING OPEN SANDWICHES

INGREDIENTS
(*Feeds 4 as a snack*)

— 2 raw medium beetroots
— 2 tsp smooth Russian
  mustard (or Dijon)
— 8 small slices rye bread,
  or a larger loaf cut into
  snack-sized pieces
— handful lettuce leaves
  (iceberg, cos, little gem –
  any are fine)
— 240g (8½oz) jar pickled
  herring
— handful fresh dill,
  finely chopped

METHOD

1. Bring a pan of water to the boil and put in the two beetroots.
   Reduce to a simmer, put the lid on and cook for about 1 hour,
   or until a knife goes easily through.

2. Leave to cool for 10 minutes then peel and grate the beetroots
   into a bowl. Drain any excess moisture away and stir in the mustard.

3. On a serving dish, layer rye bread, lettuce, a spoonful of beetroot,
   herring and dill. Vera likes to serve her sandwiches on a bed of
   lettuce too.

Grandma Phan Thị Mỹ's Seabass in Tomato and Dill Broth

Uyen Luu, food writer, photographer & supper-club host

Ingredients

— 1 tbsp cooking oil
(vegetable, sunflower
or groundnut)
— 2 shallots, sliced
— 1 clove garlic,
finely chopped
— 1.5l (6 cups) water or homemade chicken or pork stock
— 2 tomatoes, sliced
into quarters
— 1 tbsp caster sugar
— 4 tbsp premium-quality
fish sauce
— 1 wild seabass, cleaned
(ask your fishmonger to
slice it into 2.5cm/1in steaks,
and to give you the head)
— juice of 1 lime
— 20g (¾oz) fresh dill, sliced
into 1cm (½in) lengths
— 1 spring onion, sliced
— fresh chopped chillies
(optional)

For the sauce

— 1 or 2 bird's-eye chillies
— 2 tbsp premium-quality
fish sauce

My mother's mother had a round, beaming face. I always remember her smiling; the crow's feet under her eyes were so deep the scorching Vietnam sun couldn't reach their depth. She would wash herbs grown in her garden and cleaver fish on a stub of trunk under the shade of a jackfruit tree for a sweet and sour fish soup.

She'd buy the fish from a lonesome fisherman at the beach as he came onto shore. In the backdrop, a green, rusty American war tank sat abandoned, overgrown with pink and yellow flowers. After the war, the Vietnamese people suffered greatly from poverty and starvation. Despite this, I willl always remember my grandmother's smile as she handed me shells of coconuts filled with coconut water.

In an instant, lunch would be ready. Everyone at home would then squeak their freshly washed feet onto the shiny ceramic floor, sitting cross-legged as the electric fan whipped around overhead. Before serving herself, my grandmother would pick at the fish with her wooden chopsticks, dipping it onto the fish sauce and placing it into my bowl. Always give to those you love first.

When I am in desperate need of the sun, this soup reminds me of her. The sweet and sour flavours are reminiscent of joy in times of hardship and hunger. There is nothing quite like sharing such a simple, yet exhilarating meal with those you love. *'An di!'* she would say. 'Go on, eat!'

Feeds 2-3

1. It is really important to have all the ingredients prepared before the cooking process, as that won't take too long and you don't want to overcook any of the ingredients. If you're having it with steamed rice, ensure the rice is cooked beforehand.

2. On a medium heat, fry the sliced shallots until golden in 1 tbsp of oil, then add the garlic. Watch until the garlic turns golden, then set aside.

3. Pour 1.5l (6 cups) boiling water or good-quality plain chicken or pork stock into a pot, add tomatoes, sugar and fish sauce and cover with a lid. Let this come to the boil then immediately add the seabass chunks, head included. Cover. When this reaches a boil, bring the heat down to simmer for about 5 minutes. Add the fried shallot and garlic with oil and the juice of a lime. Taste to adjust the sweet, sour and salty balance, adding more sugar if a little more sweetness is needed, more lime for sour and more fish sauce for umami. To check if the fish is cooked, pierce a knife through the deepest part – if it reaches the bone easily, it is cooked.

4. On a separate plate or bowl, crush the bird's-eye chillies with the back of a spoon onto the surface then add about 2 tbsp of good-quality fish sauce to it. Take the fish out of the pan and place onto the chillies and fish sauce.

5. Pour the soup into a large sharing bowl, then add chopped dill, spring onion and fresh chillies. Serve with steamed rice.

FLORA

Flora met us off the ferry at Hvar in a generously rimmed striped straw hat and modish circular sunglasses. We walked around the bay to the home she inhabits half the year, next door to the infamous Hula Hula bar. We sashayed past with pride, in the knowledge that we were defying tourist traps and getting the fully local experience.

Our octopus came from a local chef called Car whom Flora has known since childhood. Because she was cooking for *Grand Dishes* he allowed her to buy one of his prized octopuses. Generally they're very hard to come by at this time of the season (September).

Frozen octopus cooks much quicker than fresh and it doesn't lose any flavour. Even if it's fresh, it's better to freeze it. The ice breaks the muscles down, which makes it much more tender. Usually the fishermen would also have bashed it about to break the tissue in the tentacles when it emerged from the ocean. We took ours down to the sea to finish the defrosting in salty water. Throughout the day Flora referred to it as 'octopussy', which naturally we all adopted.

On day two with Flora we embarked on a gnocchi-making session (*njoki* in Croatian). Traditionally these dumplings are the accompaniment to *pašticada*, a typical Dalmatian beef stew made with Croatian dessert wine, prunes for sweetness and cloves and nutmeg for spice. Flora's gnocchi were particularly elegant, their detailing created with a quick roll across the back of a cheese grater. Their textured nature ensures they pick up all the gravy. Flora advocated lots of parmesan to finish. We made a vegetarian version with crispy fried sage leaves from the garden and extra butter (and more parmesan).

Born: *Hvar, Croatia, 1944*
Mother tongue: *Croatian*
Grandchildren: *Luka, Flora, Xenia, Sofia*
They call her: *Nona*

I learned to make this dish almost 50 years ago. It was my uncle's recipe. He was a sailor and had only a few dishes that he could cook really well. As a sailor his repertoire was mostly fish, and he would do this octopus salad. It's actually much harder to get hold of octopus now though. Here in Hvar when I go to the fishmonger for it, sometimes it's all gone because the restaurants get the best of the catch. I have to rely on my friends to provide it. Tourism has changed Hvar and Croatia a lot in that respect.

The rest of my culinary knowledge is all from my grandmother and my mother. I learned these dishes very organically from them. I even wrote and published a book of family recipes, *The Sweet Taste of a Dalmatian Love Affair*, inspired by my grandmother Flora's handwritten recipes. It's combined with the love letters from her fiancé, Viktor, written during their long courtship while he was studying and working abroad between 1903 and 1909.

Many of the dishes my grandmother sent to Viktor carried strong allusions to physical passion and love symbolism in an era when love and passion couldn't be declared so openly. She interpreted the recipes, using her imagination to reflect the love with which the dishes were prepared. I do think it's important to have some imagination and not follow these cookbooks like the bible.

Imagination and a sense of freedom is what you need to be a good cook. I sometimes feel sorry for people who have to stick to a recipe and don't interpret recipes and dishes in their own way. That's part of the joy of cooking. I am happy that my sons and older grandchildren are developing into creative cooks. When I cook, I cook out of love. Love for cooking and a love for the person I am cooking for.

Love is different according to the man you're with. With my first husband I shared a love for our island of Hvar, history of art and literature. We lived in Zagreb and had a great group of friends that would meet regularly in our small flat. The first time I started to cook on my own was for these gatherings, punctuated with lots of wine and heated discussions. My husband was not interested in food – he could survive on poetry alone – but he understood the importance of sharing it and the atmosphere of warmth and welcoming that home-cooked dishes can create.

When he admitted to an affair I was devastated, but I tried not to be bitter and managed to maintain the normality at home for the sake of our son. Sometimes when I would hear his key turn in the door at dawn, instead of questioning his absence, I'd make a delicious breakfast and fill the house with the smell of freshly brewed coffee before leaving for work and taking our son to school.

I tried to look my best all the time. I had this idea that if he remained living at home, he would realise the value of our family life and stay with us. Although it did not work, we remain friends.

I met my second husband through our work as curators. Sometimes I tease him that his love for me and love for Dalmatia and my cooking are inseparable. There's no rule and there's no one way to love. You have to have trust and to laugh together and of course, have a passion.

If I have one lesson to pass on to my grandchildren, it is to be kind and to always try to understand. Even if someone has hurt you, you should try and see things from their perspective. Don't keep love and sentiment to yourself; always be free to express yourself and have an open dialogue.

—

Nona Flora

NONA FLORA'S CROATIAN OCTOPUS SALAD

INGREDIENTS
(*Feeds 4*)

— 1 large or 2 small frozen
   Mediterranean octopus,
   gutted
— 1 small red onion,
   peeled only
— 3 bay leaves
— 2 sprigs fresh thyme
— 1 tsp dried oregano
— handful fresh parsley
— 2 tsp black peppercorns
— 2 wine corks (optional,
   added to the cooking water
   to encourage tenderisation,
   according to Flora)

FOR THE SALAD

— 2 medium potatoes,
   peeled and halved
— 1 small red onion,
   finely chopped
— 2 plum tomatoes or 6–8
   cherry tomatoes, chopped
— small handful fresh parsley
   leaves, finely chopped
   (also good with dill!)
— 4 tbsp capers and their juice
— 3 garlic cloves,
   finely chopped
— 8 black olives, sliced
— 8 Kalamata olives, sliced
— olive oil
— balsamic or red wine vinegar

METHOD

1. Cooking octopus is simple, but if you aren't careful the texture can end up a little rubbery, so make sure to freeze yours first and follow Flora's instructions closely. Start by thawing the 'octopussy' in the fridge – Flora finished thawing hers in the sea.

2. Rinse off any grains of sand that might be left on the tentacles. Place the octopus in a large saucepan, add the whole peeled onion, all the herbs, peppercorns and the wine corks, if using. Cover with boiling water straight from the kettle and quickly bring to the boil again in the pan. As soon as it comes to the boil, immediately reduce the heat and let it gently simmer for about 40–50 minutes, until tender.

3. While it cooks, start making the salad. Pop the potatoes in the octopus water to boil for 10–15 minutes, until tender. Prepare the vegetables and lay them out separately on your chopping board, ready to layer onto a serving dish when the time comes. When the potatoes are cooled, chop them into small cubes, put them in a small bowl and dress with olive oil.

4. When the time is almost up, start testing the octopus for tenderness by pushing a fork through the thickest part of the flesh; if it slides in easily, it's done. Octopussy should be wonderfully pink: take it out of the water, admire it and leave to cool just a little.

5. It's good to dress the salad while the octopus is still warm, so slice the octopus into 0.5cm (¼in) coins and drizzle with olive oil, vinegar (Flora uses balsamic), sea salt and pepper, to taste.

6. Now start layering all the veg (the potato cubes, red onion, tomatoes, parsley, capers, garlic and olives) with the octopus, adding extra drizzles of olive oil and vinegar as you go.

7. And on the side – bread! Flora had a forgotten loaf that was a bit on the dry side, which she revived by sprinkling it with a little water and then 'bunged' in the oven to regain its past glory.

FINA

We've come to a fair few of these grandmothers through friends of friends. Fina came through our good pal Stefano. Over the course of a few weeks and months, we'd managed to contact Fina's niece (texting her in our broken Italian), who then went back and forth between Fina and her own daughter to pin down a recipe and date on which we could visit her.

Eventually we set out to road trip through Sicily across two weeks in September, three grannies in our diary. So excited were we for our granny hat-trick, that the night before meeting Fina, upon landing in Palermo, we set out for aperitivos. One negroni led to another and while one of us didn't make it home until 5 a.m., the other didn't make it back to the hotel at all.

Still, we are dedicated to our granny mission. We showed up to Nonna Fina's with time to spare, albeit a little bleary-eyed. She cared for us as our grandmothers would have, with a plateful of comfort food and a wry, knowing smile that said, 'I've been there. I know you better than you know yourselves.'

This rich, sweet-savoury pasta dish was exactly what we needed and by our second helping we'd all but forgotten our throbbing temples. The *formaggio povero* (poor man's parmesan) - essentially fried breadcrumbs - added texture and depth of flavour and was an essential finishing touch to soak up the alcohol.

Born: *Palermo, Sicily, 1951*
Mother tongue: *Italian*
Grandchildren: *Mattia, Samuele, Laura*
They call her: *Nonna*

Pasta con le sarde is such a typically Sicilian dish and it's so simple to make with a very rich flavour of the island. The breadcrumbs to accompany the dish are called *formaggio povero* because this once was the parmesan of the poor. It's also very traditional and I still like to use it instead of parmesan now because it adds great texture to the dish.

Sugo is a traditional pomodoro pasta sauce that everyone here in Italy knows how to make. I'm 'La Sugara' amongst my friends because they all want me to make my tomato sauce for them whenever I go to one of their houses. It was the first thing I learned to make and eventually, I learned to make it very well.

It wasn't always this way, though. The first time I tried to make it I was only 12 years old. I tried to cook it without adding water to my saucepan and I burned the pan. At that point in my life, my father had decided I should know how to cook. He just came home from work one day and called me into the kitchen for my first lesson. My parents both worked and my elder sister was married. I was the only girl in the house and my father thought it imperative for me to learn to cook for my brothers.

He was actually the one who taught me how to cook, not my mother. I had to prepare lunch and dinner for my five older brothers every day

and so my father taught me very early how to make some classic dishes in order to feed the family. Sometimes my uncle Toto would help too. He lived close by and I'd call him and ask him to come over and show me how to make things. So everything I learned about Sicilian cuisine was from two men, not my mother or nonna, which is usually the case here.

I have never stopped learning new things when it comes to the kitchen, though. Whenever I travel to a specific region, I learn to make a dish from that region. Instead of souvenirs, I collect the typical dishes of each of the places I have visited. I usually ask what ingredients are in each dish, then I come home and get to cooking the dish, experimenting in order to recreate the taste from memory. It's how I have so many Italian dishes in my repertoire.

For example, I'd never eaten pasta with squid ink before going to Messina and once I'd tried it, I was set on making it at home. As soon as we were back in Palermo, I asked my husband to go out and buy squid, then off I went on a mission to recreate it. It wasn't simple, but I managed to get the flavour in the end. In all these years of cooking with this trial-and-error approach, I've somehow managed to hone the skill of perfecting the taste of a dish from memory. It's so important to keep testing yourself and to keep things interesting. That's what I like to do in the kitchen. Food is so wrapped up with memories that I like to recreate these dishes as a form of nostalgia for the happy times I've had travelling.

—

Nonna Fina

NONNA FINA'S SICILIAN PASTA WITH SARDINES (*Pasta con le sarde*)

INGREDIENTS
(*Feeds 4*)

— 175g (heaped 1 cup) fennel, finely sliced
— 1 shallot, finely diced
— 3 tbsp extra virgin olive oil
— 4 tinned anchovies
— 60g (⅔ cup) raisins
— 60g (½ cup) pine nuts
— 350g (12oz) sardines, de-headed and chopped up
— 2 tbsp tomato purée
— 100ml (7 tbsp) white wine
— pinch caster sugar (optional)
— 400g (14oz) bucatini pasta
— squeeze of lemon (optional)

FOR THE POVERO CHEESE
(*crispy breadcrumbs*)

— 125g (2½ cups) breadcrumbs
— glug of olive oil

METHOD

1. Gently boil your fennel until soft (about 5 minutes) then leave in the water to soak until it's needed.

2. Fry the shallot in the oil on a medium–low heat until translucent and starting to turn golden.

3. Add the anchovies to fry with the shallot – these will almost dissolve as they cook and add a salty kick.

4. Once the anchovies have broken down, add the raisins and pine nuts, swiftly followed by the fresh sardines, tomato purée and white wine.

5. Drain your cooked fennel over a jug, reserving the water. Add the fennel to the pan.

6. Add a pinch of sugar (if using), a hefty grind of salt and black pepper. Stir your sauce to combine and use the fennel water to just cover the ingredients and bring to a simmer.

7. Turn to a low heat and cover. Once the oil has risen to the surface and the layer of foam has cleared, that's when your sauce is ready – this should take about 10–15 minutes. It should be a loose and saucy consistency.

8. When this happens, put salted water on for the pasta. Fina uses bucatini pasta – the hole running through the middle is perfect for catching the sauce, but feel free to use whichever you prefer.

9. While the pasta cooks, begin to toast the breadcrumbs in a non-stick frying pan. Add a good glug of olive oil and disperse across the breadcrumbs by stirring. Keep stirring for about 2 minutes, or until they turn golden. Season as you like.

10. When the pasta is al dente, drain and toss with the sauce and serve with a squeeze of lemon and the breadcrumbs scattered over the top.

SHARON

Our great-granny USA road trip officially kicked off in North Carolina's Outer Banks, with us driving past sand dunes and beach oats billowing in a warm breeze (because summer was just wrapping up on the Atlantic coast). We'd been tipped off on a local cooking hero, grandmother Sharon, who lives in a hurricane-battered home that has withstood 60 years of wind thrashings.

Its very beams were once trodden by sailors doomed to meet their end at Diamond Shoals - the most eastern point of the USA at which two deadly currents clash - only 10 minutes from Sharon's home.

'You just batten down and make sure as hell you have some potatoes, onions and a burner to cook with - it ain't scary at all,' is her reaction to the extreme weather she faces each year. Her stew included a 'bread pie', which is essentially chopped-up bits of bread dough cooked in broth to become flat, tender and chewy dumplings that serve to thicken the soup and add warmth to this hurricane-defying dish.

In typical fashion of people from the South, Sharon welcomed us with warm, wide arms. We relished gulping down her intelligent insights on life as much as the sweet iced tea on her back porch. We talked politics, philosophy and love as we crowded over her stove to cook up stewed shrimp, caught fresh on her doorstep that day.

Born: *Outer Banks, North Carolina, USA, 1956*
Mother tongue: *American English*
Grandchildren: *Lilyauna, Wesley, Aurora*
They call her: *Grandmother*

One of our little laughs is that we'd rather have a foot of tide here in the Outer Banks than an inch of snow. Hatteras Island is where I grew up. It's the most eastern point of the whole of the USA and we're famous here for the sheer amount of ships that have met their end on these shores.

My dad was a fisherman and we grew up on seafood. As a young child, stewed shrimp was always so delicious. I learned to cook with my father and his mother, my grandmother. This was her recipe to begin with and has been passed down to me. We make this stew because it makes sense in this part of the world. People come here

to Hatteras from all over to fish. I'm only just now learning how to make meat dishes. I crave a clam and a shrimp more than I ever have a fried pork chop or a hamburger.

What I think is a real shame about what has happened to the area isn't our extreme weather - it's this over-tourism that is happening all over the world now. We used to fish to feed ourselves and to feed our families, but what's happening in Hatteras is this over-commercialisation of everything. If I take you down to Diamond Shoals - where all these shipwrecks have happened over the years and where my father used to fish - you'll just see hundreds of men in four by fours

who've come here for a fishing competition. We can't even fish in our own waters any more because it's seen to be more profitable to let these people (most of them supporting our current president, who I like to call Mad Max) pillage the waters. It's just not fair. Tourism and capitalism is slowly eroding all that is characteristic of really individual places like Cape Hatteras.

I suppose I'm very opinionated for someone that lives around these parts. Men don't expect women to be so opinionated. I never wanted to be married. My mantra was 'unattainable and untrainable – I'll be your friend longer than your lover'. I just didn't trust men. I didn't want to marry someone who thought they owned me and I'd 'better have supper on at five or else'. I didn't want to take care of kids while they're out gallivanting with their buddies. I'm a person too. I knew men who were very demeaning to their wives and I just didn't want that part. I knew life could be lived very culturally. I love men – don't get me wrong – but they frightened me. They would have affairs and then expect to keep their wife (who would just stay silent). It just seemed all wrong to me.

It's pretty crazy living conditions here because of the hurricanes and the floods we're hit with each year, but I live here because I like to feel exhilarated. All the houses are raised each year, so they're all on these kind of stilts we call pilots. They were on the ground at one point and now they're being raised many feet above the ground to protect them from the flooding. They did the same thing with Cape Hatteras lighthouse. They moved an entire lighthouse down the road. Hurricane season ain't scary though. We just batten down the hatches, make sure we have some gas lamps and heaters and plenty of potatoes, and we get by.

That's where this stew comes from. The shrimp is obviously easy to come by here on the island and then we thicken the whole thing out with these hearty potatoes and the bread pie crust. It's a dish designed to really fill you up. Comfort food when the weather is thrashing our homes and giving it all it's got. If you want a real good feed, you add more potatoes and more dumplings.

—

Grandmother Sharon

GRANDMOTHER SHARON'S OUTER BANKS SHRIMP STEW WITH 'PIE BREAD'

INGREDIENTS
(Feeds 4)

— 3 tbsp olive oil
— 500g (1lb) shelled king
   prawns
— 4 waxy red potatoes,
   skin on and cut into 2cm
   (¾in) cubes
— ½ large white onion, diced
— 1 tsp sea salt
— 2 spring onions, chopped

FOR THE PIE BREAD

— 120g (1 cup) plain flour
— 1 tbsp butter

FOR THE PICKLED LETTUCE

— 1 romaine lettuce,
   finely shredded
— 100ml (7 tbsp) cider vinegar
— 100ml (7 tbsp) water

METHOD

1. Start with the pie bread. Combine the ingredients in a bowl, rubbing the butter into the flour with your hands. Season with salt and pepper and slowly add cold water a tiny bit at a time (around 60ml/¼ cup). Mix as you go and stop adding water when the flour firms up and comes together into a ball, but isn't sticky or wet. Knead for 1 minute and set aside with a tea towel over the top of the bowl as you prepare the rest.

2. Next shred your lettuce and mix in a bowl with the vinegar and water. Set aside in the fridge to pickle.

3. Now for the stew: place a large pan over a medium heat with the olive oil (enough to cover the base of the pan) and cook half of the shrimp until pink and perhaps turning slightly golden at the edges. Remove with a slotted spoon and set aside.

4. Put the second batch in the same pan, cook for 1 minute and add the potatoes, onion and sea salt along with a sprinkling of pepper. Pour in enough water to cover all the ingredients, bring to a boil, reduce to a simmer and cook for 10 minutes, or until the potatoes are almost tender.

5. While the stew cooks, return to the pie bread. Dust a clean surface with flour and roll out your dough 3mm (⅛in) thick. Cut the dough into 3cm (1¼in) squares.

6. When the stew has cooked for 10 minutes, lay the pieces of pie bread into the pan, cover and cook for 15 minutes on a very low heat, stirring occasionally, until the pastry is tender and puffed and the stew has thickened slightly. Top up the broth with water if it's not soupy enough for you.

7. Ladle into bowls, drop in the tender prawns from the first batch and sprinkle with spring onion. Serve the pickled lettuce on the side.

DAGMAR

Dagmar sent a boat for us. We raced across the bay to Palmižana island in Croatia with ear-to-ear grins. A battered, chugging Land Rover took us up the hill, deeper and deeper into a botanical playground. It dropped us at the top of the path down to the Meneghello home - bright red and royal blue, covered with bold art, rosemary bushes, olive and orange trees between mad, giant cacti. Dagmar's family bought the island in 1906 and slowly created a paradise, importing the cacti from Mexico.

Dagmar cooked her *gregada* stew on an open flame. Two tanned males got a menacing fire going in a matter of seconds upon her command. It also works fine on high heat on the hob. Any white fish will work; it's just very important that it's super-fresh. Dagmar used red scorpionfish (traditionally associated with bouillabaisse), grouper fish, big shrimp and clams.

Eight women ate at a red and blue table overlooking the sea, including two of Dagmar's best friends - a cool, red-headed artist and a beautiful befreckled jewellery designer who exalted the power of female friendships and believed that 'women are simply on another dimension'.

Born: *Ruma, Serbia, 1943*
Mother tongue: *Croatian*
Grandchildren: *Giorgio, Pave, Toni, Matteo, Alma, Stella, Elia, Luče*
They call her: *Baka*

I'm now an old lady, but I first made this in 1965. When I first came here, to the island of Palmižana, my husband thought he'd also found himself a cook, but I really wasn't well at all. From the very beginning, I had an awful time. There was no electricity and no running water when I first arrived. I always said the best language I could speak at the time was dog language, because the only people I had to talk to weren't actually people, they were dogs.

I'd lived in Zagreb, was the daughter of the county mayor, and a successful journalist, but I'd fallen in love. On Palmižana then, we had no taxi boats to ferry us back and forth to Hvar or Split, but I couldn't live without him.

I ran away from the island five times but I realised life without him wasn't bearable.

He was a very attractive man, my husband. When you saw him, your mouth would drop open and you'd catch yourself salivating. He was a very successful fisherman. He would dive down to 30 metres with no breathing equipment and was known after the Second World War as a champion freediver. In 1954 there was a book written about sports fishermen and they came here and featured my husband. He caught grouper.

We started with a small generator for electricity and we built everything from scratch. My father and I planted all the cacti that populate the island. He was a botanist and brought it all back from Latin America with him. We always had fresh food on the island because it was all that was available to us. We had to fish for fresh fish because we had no way of preserving it or keeping things for days. I started making *gregada* because of all the fish he would bring back. Fresh fish needs as little cooking as possible. When I came here, my husband was the best cook and I learned from him, actually. We would cook it together with fishermen friends of his.

For *gregada*, you must have all the ingredients fresh on the day. You can't cook it with fish from an icebox. If you're cooking this, ensure that your clams, your fish – everything is sourced on the day. There are not a lot of complex spices or herbs, the fresh fish and the shell of the prawns and the clams gives it a lovely taste of the sea. It's a famous dish here for us on Palmižana. Amra, the artist staying here with me right now, has even painted a beautiful painting of *gregada* for us.

I've had artist friends to stay from the very start of my time here. In the winter, we sometimes would have three or four months not seeing anyone and I would get so lonely, so I began to invite my friends to stay for a month or so at a time. The island would become a sanctuary to them and they would paint. That's why the place is filled with art. I've become one of Croatia's biggest collectors because of it. I love the way that artists have come from all over and really painted a feeling of Palmižana, most of the time leaving their work behind here on the island.

These paintings are not only paintings. People are coming here and they're taking soul from this place. When we all die, these works of art will remain, and that is a very nice and comforting thought. I have a similar feeling with special recipes, like my *gregada*. Every dish you cook and make is like a painting; you start with some raw ingredients but you can end with something truly beautiful and expressive. It stirs emotion.

—

Baka Dagmar

BAKA DAGMAR'S CROATIAN FISH AND POTATO STEW (*Gregada*)

INGREDIENTS
(*Feeds 4-6*)

— 12 tbsp olive oil approx.,
  plus more for serving
— 3 medium potatoes,
  sliced into 0.5cm (¼in)
  rounds
— 2 small/medium onions,
  sliced into thin rings
— 2 garlic cloves, sliced
  into thin slivers
— ½ bunch fresh parsley,
  leaves chopped
— 500-600g (approx. 1lb)
  mixed white fish and
  seafood of your choice
  (Dagmar used red
  scorpionfish, grouper fish,
  king prawns and clams)
— 300ml (1¼ cups) dry white
  wine

METHOD

1. Cut any larger fillets of fish into chunks and set aside.

2. In a flat-bottomed, low-sided pan drizzle in some olive oil. Layer the potatoes on the bottom of the pan, then drizzle with a little more olive oil and a sprinkle of salt.

3. Layer the onion rings on top of the potatoes, then drizzle with olive oil and sprinkle with salt again.

4. Scatter the garlic over, followed by a small handful of parsley. Next add the fish and another handful of parsley.

5. Pour over another generous drizzle of olive oil and the white wine. Top up with boiling water so that the fish is still visible above – you can make it more soupy by adding more liquid if you like, but Dagmar likes just a small amount of broth.

6. Cook uncovered on a very high heat for 20 minutes, or until the potatoes are soft. Don't be tempted to stir it in case you break up the potatoes and fish. Instead, just give it a shake from time to time to ensure the potatoes aren't sticking to the bottom of the pan.

7. After 20 minutes the sauce should have reduced. Check the sauce for seasoning and add salt if it needs it.

8. Serve in individual bowls, topped with the remaining parsley, a grind of black pepper and a drizzle of olive oil.

MEAT

BETSY

On the odd occasion we've been privy to grandmothers cooking with their own grandchildren, witnessing the passing-on of skills, recipes and traditions from withered, wrinkled hands to tiny ones not yet trusted to hold a knife alone. Such was the case at Betsy's in Mexico City.

With the patience of a saint, Betsy took to the chopping board with seven-year-old Bella to chop an onion, teaching her how to take proper hold of a knife, the technique she uses to slice and finely dice. One deft move for her, a great deal of concentration for Bella. Still, it has taken Betsy a lifetime to perfect. What struck us was the gentleness with which grandmother taught granddaughter, a willingness to spend time that perhaps parents aren't lucky enough to afford their own children.

We ate for hours, alternating between rice and crispy tostadas as a base for our spicy chicken and spoonfuls of black beans, no real rush to leave the table. It was here that we learned the term *sobremesa*, the ultimate dining experience, in which Mexicans hang out at the table from lunch until dinner, filling the space between with leftovers, snacks and conversation.

Born: *Mexico City, Mexico, 1944*
Mother tongue: *Mexican*
Grandchildren: *Sofie, Bella*
They call her: *Abuela*

Every room in my apartment here in Mexico City has its own view. I love to look over the vastness of my city. The only problem with our houses is that they're not built for the cold, so we freeze in winter here. I've always lived in Mexico City. I was born here and now I'm old.

What has always been a part of the way I dine is the concept of *sobremesa*. It's the Mexican tradition of spending hours and hours at the table. Even between meals we will stay at the table and snack. It's something I've done since I was a little girl at my own grandmother's house. For this reason, I always have many snacks here.

We also have strong breakfasts in Mexico. We love our proteins and cheese, chicken, eggs and beans feature quite heavily in a Mexican breakfast. Not forgetting tortilla. We make *chilaquiles* and have a bowl of fruit after that, as well as our coffee and sweet bread. My grandmother loved combining sweet and savoury things, so my breakfast always has a good selection of both. We Mexicans really love our food. We can eat *tingas de pollo quesadilla* for breakfast too. So this dish can move from breakfast to lunch and dinner.

My mother would make *tingas de pollo* and I loved it so much I've been making it for many years. My granddaughters now have also taken a liking to it, so it's a classic dish I always cook for the family. It's so simple but very full of flavour and goodness. It's also very typical of Mexican cuisine. I can barely remember when I first made it. I make it one time a week, minimum. I learned to make this dish with

157

my mother. I was so young, probably as young as my grand-daughter Isabella is now, around eight years old. I loved to cook and so she began to involve me in the cooking process.

I went to go and study to become a teacher for young elementary school children, but because I loved cooking so much, I started teaching my daughters and their friends at home how to cook. I combined both of my passions and become a teacher of the culinary arts. Now my daughter has her own culinary school, no doubt because of these forma-tive years. It makes me feel very proud. Cooking is happiness for me and I'm pleased my daughters and granddaughters can draw the same joy from it.

Everything has changed here in Mexico City since I was young. Everyone is much more educated. That's life though - in general, it always changes. Nothing can be expected to stay the same. Ten years ago I was walking down the street here in the neighbourhood and I fell in the street, between all the cars and moving traffic. I couldn't get up and it was

terrifying because it was such a busy road. I fractured so many bones and had so many operations, I could barely move at the end of it all. It changed everything in my life. I was awful physically. I need to use a cane now to walk. I call it Mundo. My husband was called Mundo. It's my support now and he was back then.

I met a woman in a store when I first had the cane and felt quite self-conscious about it, and she had told me in passing that her grandchildren call her cane 'Mario', after her husband. So I said in response, 'I should call mine "Mundo".' Then we both walked out of the store speaking to our canes - '*Vamonos* [let's go],' we said to them, and walked off with the new incarnation of our husbands. We have to have some humour with these things.

—

Abuela Betsy

ABUELA BETSY'S MEXICAN CHICKEN TOSTADAS

INGREDIENTS
(Feeds 4-6)

— 1 tsp olive oil
— ½ large onion, diced
— 2 garlic cloves
— 4 chicken breasts
— 8 soft tortillas (preferably corn), cut into small discs
— 200g (1 cup) cottage cheese or sour cream

FOR THE SAUCE

— 7 plum tomatoes, chopped into quarters
— ½ large onion, roughly chopped
— 4 garlic cloves, roughly chopped
— 2 chipotle chillies from a tin, or 2 tsp chipotle paste
— 1 tbsp olive oil
— 1 onion, cut in half and sliced into half-moons

FOR THE REFRIED BEANS

— 1 tsp olive oil
— ½ large onion, diced
— 2 x 400g (14oz) tins black beans

METHOD

1. Put a medium-sized pan on medium heat and add the olive oil. Soften the onion and garlic, about 8 minutes, and add the chicken breasts. Stir and brown a little.

2. Add a pinch of salt to the pan and follow with enough water to just cover the chicken. Put the lid on and cook for around 40 minutes. Skim off any foam that gathers on the top.

3. Meanwhile, make the sauce. Pulse the tomatoes, onion, garlic and chipotle chillies or paste in a blender – do it in two batches if you need to, adding a little water if necessary. The result should be thinner than a smoothie, more like a spicy tomato juice.

4. Heat the oil in a non-stick pan. Hold a sieve over the pan and pour the tomato sauce in. Use a spoon to push the sauce through the sieve to remove skin and seeds. Add the sliced onion, season to taste, stir and let simmer for 20 minutes.

5. While the chicken and sauce both simmer away, start preparing your tostadas. Use a cookie cutter to cut discs, around 8–10cm (3–4in), out of your tortillas – as many as you can. Lay out on a baking tray and brush with olive oil. Set aside and turn the oven on to 200°C/180°C fan/400°F/gas 6.

6. When the chicken is done, remove it from the water. Leave until cool enough to handle, then shred and add to the sauce.

7. For the beans: soften the onion in the oil in a medium saucepan for 8 minutes on a medium heat, then add the beans and their liquid and bring to the boil, then lower to a simmer for 20 minutes, stirring occasionally, until liquid has reduced a bit.

8. Once the beans are soft, remove from the heat and use a potato masher to mash the beans until smooth and creamy. Taste and season – and don't worry if the mixture is a touch runny; once you've left it to cool slightly the beans will thicken more.

9. While the beans cook, pop the tostadas in the oven for 8 minutes, or until crisp and slightly golden.

10. Transfer everything to serving dishes and lay out for your guests to assemble: smear a tostada with refried beans, followed with a spoonful of chicken and topped with a dollop of cottage cheese or sour cream (Betsy uses panella cheese or *queso fresco*).

ESTER

Driving to Haifa from Tel Aviv on an empty stomach was good advice from Roni, granddaughter of Ester. She knew her grandmother, in true Georgian style, would put on a lavish feast. Ester lives in a block of apartments, her flat neighbouring her family's own home. Just two front doors separate her from her son, daughter-in-law and grandchildren, so while we cooked, the entire family would pop in and out to grab various bits from the kitchen or just to get a glimpse of their granny in action.

We usually ask for one dish from each grandmother, but Ester was one of the ladies that went overboard on her food prep. We whizzed around after her, trying to measure flour as she 'felt' the amount she'd need to make *khachapuri*, a traditional Georgian cheese bread (so indulgent and delicious). We handled animal intestines as she expertly stuffed them with aromatically spiced meat for perhaps the biggest sausage we have ever had the pleasure of holding. We watched as she blitzed the most obscene amount of garlic into a paste for a chicken dish that is definitely best reserved for any night but date night.

Lunch was served next door with the rest of the family, where we took up residence at a huge banqueting-style table, 10 of us sharing from enormous platters placed across its length. A rowdy, playful and laughter-filled lunch that saw grandchildren tease grandma, laugh at her stories and at times become unexpectedly quiet to catch an anecdote they hadn't yet heard.

Born: *Georgia, 1950*
Mother tongue: *Georgian*
Grandchildren: *Roni, Yuval, Tomer, Maya, Tami, Jossi, Odel*
They call her: *Bebi*

I came to Israel when I was 21 and left my mother behind in Georgia. It was only then that I started to cook. I had no need to before that because my mother would take care of everything in the kitchen. It was just from watching my mother deliver these incredible feasts on a daily basis that I gleaned my culinary know-how. This dish was one my mother would make often, and it reminds me of the home I grew up in. I've never been back to Georgia since I left. What was my home city has now become a part of Russia. It no longer exists, sadly.

Cooking is important in life because it is a preservation of your tradition. It isn't just for the sake of putting food on the table for our loved ones, but for remembering our mothers and our grandmothers. It was crucial to me to cook as my mother did so that I could feel her closer to me. I also want my family, my children and grandchildren to really know Georgian food. When I cook Georgian food, my past comes to me and the people from my past, too.

I was just 12 when I met my husband, and he was 20. I know this is not the done thing now. He wanted me a lot more than I wanted him. In fact, I threw an entire bottle of water on him when we first met and he made clear his intentions. I was far too young, so at the beginning I really didn't want to get married. He was handsome, but I wanted to go to school. Still, it was really essential for me to marry another Jew and my family were happy with him, so that's how it happened for me. He had just seen me and then asked my father for the OK. Our family were very religious.

I didn't end up going to school, of course. Let's say I attended the school of life. I was cooking for a family in my early 20s. I was just lucky to have found someone that was as sociable as I am. Alexander loved travelling and having guests over. He kept life interesting. When he died, the lights went out for me, but I am trying to live on. I keep cooking and working and I just keep going for the family.

When I moved from Georgia to Israel, it was just my husband and I. I felt completely alone because we had to leave everyone behind. The ideology was what brought us here, the idea that finally there would be a place where we would 'belong'. The Israeli dream. We were excited to come, but on arrival it was not what I expected.

I came from a communist country to a capitalist country and it wasn't what I was used to. We started absolutely from scratch and had nothing. We were rich in Georgia, but coming into Israel, we couldn't bring anything with us. My gold and any valuables were all left behind. The Georgian government wouldn't allow us to take anything with us. What we had earned in the country, we had to leave behind. It was so mentally challenging to go from running a restaurant and owning a business to having nothing.

When we arrived, my husband worked as a builder, laying the roads of Israel. It was very hard work and we went from being very rich to incredibly poor. We knew it would be difficult, but we didn't imagine just how many financial difficulties we'd have in our new, promised land. I also only knew a couple of words in Hebrew. At the time, the Jews that came in from Europe were the best Jews in the hierarchy and those Jews coming from the Middle East were seen as the lowest level of Jew. It's still very much like this now. The Europeans are seen as better. I really do believe that love, respect and kindness are the most important characteristics a person should have in life. We could all do with a little bit more of each.

—

Bebi Ester

BEBI ESTER'S GEORGIAN CHICKEN WITH WALNUT SAUCE AND POLENTA

INGREDIENTS
(Feeds 4-6)

— 6 chicken thighs
— 2 tbsp rapeseed oil
— 600ml (2½ cups) chicken or
  vegetable stock
— 300g (scant 2 cups) quick
  polenta

FOR THE WALNUT SAUCE

— 1 small onion, diced
— 1 tsp rapeseed oil
— 400g (3⅓ cups) walnuts
— 4 cloves garlic
— 1 tbsp curry powder
— 1 tsp chilli flakes
— 1 tsp salt
— 1 tsp white pepper

METHOD

1. Preheat oven to 220°C/200°C fan/425°F/gas 7. Place the chicken in a baking tray, drizzle with the oil and season, rubbing all over to coat.

2. Roast in the oven for 30 minutes, or until cooked through and golden on top. Remove and set aside.

3. Next pour the stock into a large saucepan and bring to the boil. Add the polenta in a thin stream, stirring continuously until it thickens, about 2–3 minutes.

4. Take off the heat, cover with a lid and leave the polenta to swell and absorb more of the stock.

5. Now make the walnut sauce: fry the onion in a little oil for 7 minutes until softened and golden at the edges. Set aside.

6. Blitz the walnuts and garlic in a blender until they form a wet paste. Transfer to a bowl and stir in the curry powder, chilli, salt and pepper.

7. Wet your hand and squeeze and massage the walnuts for about 10 minutes. They'll become smoother as you manipulate them. Some oil may begin to show – if it does, drain it off and save to drizzle over the final dish.

8. Add the walnut mix back into the blender with the onion and turn on. Slowly add water until it's a liquidy consistency, a bit thicker than double cream – about 400ml (1¾ cups), but you may need a bit more.

9. Put the sauce in a pan, bring to the boil and simmer for 5 minutes. Stir the chicken thighs into the sauce with all the chicken juices (really scrape the tray to get all the cooking juices in). Cook for 15 minutes and test the seasoning.

10. Serve with the polenta and a veg of your choice.

Tip: For added flavour, use 400ml (1¾ cups) chicken or vegetable stock instead of water when you add the walnuts back to the blender.

Nani Leela Mattoo's Kashmiri Rogan Josh
Devina Seth, restaurateur

Ingredients

— 2 tbsp mustard oil
— ¼ tsp cumin seeds
— 2 bay leaves
— 1 medium onion,
  thinly sliced
— 2 black cardamom pods
— 4 cloves
— 2 pieces cinnamon
— 1 star anise
— 2 tsp red chilli powder
— 600g (1lb 5oz) chicken
  breast, roughly cubed
— 2cm (¾in) piece fresh
  ginger, grated
— ½ tsp ground ginger
— pinch asafoetida
— 2 tbsp plain yoghurt
  or Greek yoghurt
— 1½ tsp fennel powder
— 1 tsp garam masala
— 1 tbsp ghee (optional)

My grandmother, who I lovingly called Nani, was the kindest, gentlest and most nurturing person I have ever known. Her wonderful qualities manifested in her food. She was a homemaker but had a scholarly, almost enlightened aura because she was so well read, aching to know more about everything around her, which made it easy for her to connect with all generations in the family.

My fondest memories with her are our early morning conversations right before I headed off to school. She would make me the most delicious omelette and share her tea with me and we would chat about friends, books, teachers and poke fun at family members.

Rogan josh was a treat and would be cooked on Sundays or at parties, and I don't think the taste ever changed. Nani would feed all of us kids from a massive plate where a huge portion of rogan josh would be mixed with fluffy white rice. She would do it while narrating a new story every time. I can close my eyes and still smell the onions caramelising with all of the whole spices. I miss her very much.

Feeds 4

1. Heat the mustard oil in a deep-bottomed pan with a lid. Mustard oil takes a little time to heat up, so as soon as you see vapours rising, it is ready.

2. Add the cumin seeds and bay leaves.

3. Once the cumin crackles, add the onion and fry until golden brown

4. Next add all the dry spices – black cardamom, cloves, cinnamon and star anise – and stir to bind.

5. Turn the heat down and add the chilli powder; be careful not to burn it.

6. Add the chicken pieces and keep cooking until it changes colour.

7. Add the grated ginger, ginger powder and asafoetida.

8. Blend the yoghurt in a bowl with the fennel powder and garam masala, plus 120ml (½ cup) of water.

9. Add the yoghurt mix to the chicken with a pinch of salt, stir to combine, turn up the heat and put the lid on the pan.

10. Once boiling, turn down low and cook until the chicken is cooked – the meat will be tender and the oil will rise to the top of the curry.

11. Stir in some ghee (optional) and your curry is ready.

CLARA MARIA

We've been lucky enough to stay overnight with a grandmother we're cooking with on a few occasions. Clara Maria kindly offered to host us for a weekend at her beautiful home on the outskirts of Madrid. Upon arrival, we sat out in the garden to wait for Clara Maria with an aperitif of beers and olives.

Soon enough she emerged from the house, a lady of such grace and class that we barely noticed the cane she needed to support her weight as she moved towards us in greeting. She sat herself down ever so slowly and cracked open a beer. From this moment, we knew we'd all get along.

We spent a weekend tirelessly listening to Clara Maria. We did have the option to head out and explore Madrid but chose instead to spend most of our time curled up on her couch near a roaring fire, absorbing stories of her times as part of the culinary set of the 1950s with Elizabeth David and Julia Child. Soaking up her views on life. Letting her positivity, her belief in following insticts, sink into our very own philosophies. All between exquisite dishes that exemplified the elegance and finesse that Clara Maria herself embodies.

Born: *Madrid, Spain, 1930*
Mother tongue: *Spanish*
Grandchildren: *Alvaro, Jacobo, Enrique, Felipe, Camila, Primi, Luis, Lorenzo, Guillermo, Eugenia, Jimena, Antonio, Clara, Sofia, Lino, Martta, Isabel*
They call her: *Yaya*

You can *escabeche* anything, from partridge and game to chicken, it's a popular classic with all the Spaniards. The verb *escabechar* in Spanish simply means to cook and preserve in vinegar, which I like to do a lot, but using only very good-quality Spanish vinegar.

Cooking with vinegar is actually one of the first lessons I taught at the Culinary Institute in New York. I had taken six Spanish chefs with me to teach a lesson on Spanish cuisine. They were very young and had never been to New York before, so I wasn't convinced they would make the early start. I said, 'Tomorrow at 7 a.m. you are here or I will come and throw a cold jar of water over your heads as you sleep.' They said, 'Of course, we will be there,' and of course, they never arrived.

Everyone at the institute was very angry, so I took the class myself to entertain them. I taught them how to do a vinaigrette with Spanish sweet sherry and sweet vinegar. You must mix half a bottle of a very good vinegar with a bottle of sweet sherry and you leave it to boil until it reduces, then let it cool, and you bottle it again for a delicious vinaigrette. They made that vinegar with a vintage that had 160 years in a bodega and a very valuable sherry. It was 100 times better than the modern vinegar in America. Cheaper as well as better.

When I got back to Spain, the bodegas behind the sherry and vinegar I had recommended were waiting for me with tons of flowers. They said that for the first time in 30 years they had sold all their stock in New York. It was because I'd taken the class for people who owned restaurants and hotels. I was so amused because I only took the class because the Spanish chefs with me had all disappeared.

Eventually I founded Alambique, a culinary school and shop in Madrid after being inspired by what I had seen of the culinary scene in New York. I was a very good friend of Elizabeth David in London, so I asked her advice when I was thinking about doing it and she was very enthusiastic about it. Then in the States I became a very good friend of Julia Childs. We were all in the same group of 'foodies', as you say now.

All my friends back home were telling me, 'You're crazy - what are you doing? We have cooks in our houses, why do we need to learn to cook?' The first month, only four people came into our shop, but I didn't mind a lot. As women, we should really trust our instincts. You live with your mind and your heart and you must cook some-thing up that is good with them. My friends were terrified, but I wasn't worried at all because I believed in what I was doing.

I think one of the best secrets of life is to just be a good person. You receive so much just by being good. You will be very happy. It's so important to have faith in whatever you go into. You must believe in what you do, very much. You have to believe it is going to happen. That's why I made a success of Alambique, because I truly believed in it. It's a question of character. Sometimes, you do something and you think, Oh I am crazy, this is ridiculous, I'm going to lose everything. But if you are sure of what you're doing, it's magic. It opens all the doors. All you must do is believe.

—

Yaya Clara Maria

YAYA CLARA MARIA'S SPANISH CHICKEN MARINATED IN SHERRY VINEGAR (*Escabeche*)

INGREDIENTS
(*Feeds 4-6*)

- 100ml (7 tbsp) olive oil
- 500g (1lb) skin-on chicken: thighs, legs or breasts (whatever you prefer)
- 1 onion, sliced into 3mm (⅛in) half-moons
- ½ bulb garlic, cloves peeled and roughly chopped
- 1 carrot, peeled and sliced in 3mm (⅛in) rounds
- 125ml (½ cup) good-quality sherry vinegar
- 400ml (1¾ cups) chicken stock
- 1 tsp black peppercorns
- 4 cloves
- 2 fresh bay leaves
- 2 sprigs fresh thyme

METHOD

1. Heat the olive oil in a non-stick sauté pan.

2. When the oil is hot, fry the chicken skin-down in the oil until browned (around 8–12 minutes), then fry the underside for 2 minutes. Remove and set aside.

3. Add the onion, garlic and carrot to the oil and fry on a medium heat for 10 minutes, or until soft but not browned.

4. Return the chicken to the pan and add the vinegar and chicken stock to cover the meat. Add the peppercorns, cloves, bay leaves and thyme and simmer for 20 minutes with the lid on.

5. Keep in the pan or move to an earthenware or ceramic dish, ensuring the meat is covered with the juices. Allow to cool, cover and then put in the fridge.

6. Refrigerate overnight and eat the next day – the flavour of the pickling liquid will mellow and the meat will tenderise. *Escabeche* lasts for up to a week, and the taste of the sherry vinegar softens more over time.

7. Serve hot or cold alongside buttery boiled new potatoes or crusty bread and pickles.

TIGGER

We were introduced to Tigger through her artist daughter, Charlotte. Tigger lived in London's trendy Hackney neighbourhood way before people ponced around with rolled-up jeans, pink socks, takeaway coffees and Danish buns. Her house was modest and cosy with loads of books, African artefacts and a neat line of framed photos of each of her 16 grandchildren in the hall.

We went to visit Tigger for an introductory cup of tea and ginger biscuit. It was a little awkward; we were nervous. Tigger wasn't sure. She kept saying, 'But I haven't had a career and I just improvise with whatever food I happen to have available.' We sat on the sofa, Tigger opposite in a chair. Within the hour, slightly over the tea limit, something clicked and we ended up squeezed together on the sofa with a photo album, Tigger exclaiming, 'It's like we're on a bus!' We set a date for two weeks later.

Tigger had painted the wall behind her white Aga a deep Yves Klein blue. She told nearly all her stories leaning against it, reboiling the kettle for more tea. Iska had a pink wig with her for a party that evening. At some moment it felt right that Tigger should try it on, and so she stood, reciting stories with such sincerity, with a bright pink bob.

Born: *London, UK, 1934*
Mother tongue: *English*
Grandchildren: *Milo, Pia, Georgia, Francis, Ella, Finbar, Louis, Johnnie, Mungo, Sam, Emily, Magda, Bruno, Olive, Joe, Minnie*
They call her: *Tigger*

We first went to Uganda when I was 24, with two babies aged 18 months and eight weeks. My husband Tim had been called up for military service and we discovered that he could do three years in the colonial service instead, so off we went.

He worked as part of a team of three doctors looking after West Nile District, a place the size of Wales. Every Monday, at the hospital, all the patients in their beds would be wheeled outside so that the wards could be hosed down – there were no windows or doors, so chickens and all sorts could just wander in. Any chickens caught inside the ward would go into the peanut stew for the patients' lunch. This was my first encounter with this recipe, which has been part of our family life ever since.

When we lived in Tanzania I was very depressed as I had little to do and was surrounded by so much poverty. In our district, there was a great scarcity of iodine in the water and many women had goitres, which meant they risked giving birth to children with disabilities. There were boxes of iodine-oil capsules stored in the hospital, and Tim suggested that we use our Land Rover to deliver them. So began an incredible adventure that took me to amazing places – through villages, up mountain passes, across rivers, which we had to ford with the capsule boxes on our heads – and some really scary driving.

Hospitality is very important, and in each village, sometimes three in a day, we would be fed –

often peanut stew - by people who could scarcely afford to feed themselves. Spices were sold in the markets in the tiniest plastic bags with just enough of each spice for a single meal. It was all most villagers could afford. Seeing people who haven't got any food makes me wild about the way people buy food and then waste it. You learn to treasure food when you see others who don't have enough. Each night as I snuggled into bed, I would think, Why was I born in England with so much, and not here with so little?

I learned a lot in Africa - most importantly, respect for the way other people live. In Malawi, there were quite a few beggars in our town. One man we regularly saw wore only half a shirt. I decided to give him some underpants, but he wore them on his head, or absolutely anywhere except where they were designed for. Who was I to say where they should be worn?

In many ways Tim dictated what I did with my life, but I would not have had it any other way. Without him, I would not have found myself in the Tanzanian mountains dining in the huts of local people, or living on the beautiful shore of the Shire River in Malawi. He changed the course of my life and I happily let him. Throughout our life together he would grow restless and decide to change everything and off we would go. I cannot imagine how I did it, but I just held hands with him and ran.
—

Tigger

TIGGER'S AFRICAN-INSPIRED PEANUT CHICKEN STEW

INGREDIENTS
(*Feeds 4-6*)

— 1 tsp coriander seeds
— 1 tsp cumin seeds
— 8 chicken thighs (Tigger
prefers skinless for this dish)
— 5 whole cloves
— 3 tbsp natural yoghurt
— 1½ tbsp olive oil
— 1 onion, diced
— 4cm (1½in) ginger, finely chopped
— 1 garlic clove, finely chopped
— ½ red chilli, finely chopped
— zest of ½ lemon
— 500ml (2 cups) chicken stock
— 2 red peppers, roughly chopped
into large pieces
— 2 tbsp smooth peanut butter
(with no added sugar)

METHOD

1. Grind the coriander and cumin in a pestle and mortar. Put the chicken in a bowl with the coriander and cumin, cloves and yoghurt, rubbing to make sure all the meat is coated. Cover and leave to marinate in the fridge for 30 minutes.

2. When the chicken has almost had long enough in the marinade, heat the olive oil in a sauté pan and add the onion to soften for 5 minutes, followed by the ginger, garlic and chilli. Continue to cook for 3 minutes, until the aromas release.

3. Add the chicken to sear all over, then add the lemon zest and chicken stock and simmer on a low heat for 20 minutes.

4. Next add the red peppers and peanut butter. Stir and cook for a final 10 minutes. Check for seasoning before serving with fluffy basmati rice boiled with a couple of cardamom pods.

Grandmother Doña Margarita's Mexican Rice with Chicken Offal (*Arroz de Novios*)

Enrique Olvera, chef

Ingredients

- 3 garlic cloves, chopped in half
- 1 onion, sliced
- 80g (3oz) fresh parsley, chopped
- pinch nutmeg
- 1 chicken stock cube dissolved in 125ml (½ cup) water
- 250g (9oz) chicken livers
- 250g (9oz) chicken sweet-breads (make sure to wash them very well and cut them into little pieces for rapid cooking, and if you can't get them, use 500g/1lb chicken livers)
- 2 bay leaves
- 1 tsp cracked black pepper
- ½ tsp turmeric
- 1 tsp dried oregano (preferably from Tabasco, Mexico!)
- 450g (2¼ cups) rice, washed and drained

My grandmother, Margarita, was a caring woman from Tabasco, in the south-east of Mexico. I never cooked *arroz de novios* with her. Her recipe was, of course, delicious but the most important thing for me is what it still represents; a dish to celebrate and share with loved ones.

To me, the rice in this dish makes it one of those dishes that feeds the soul. Although it's really not just about the dish itself, it's the ceremony that goes with it. It reminds me of a loving grandma, the people I once shared her table with and the perfect smell and texture chicken offal gives to the plate. This whole experience is one of the memories with my grandmother I cherish the most.

Feeds 6

1. In a large pot, heat the oil on medium heat and stir-fry the garlic and onion. When the onion turns clear, add the chopped parsley (save some for garnish) and take off the heat.

2. Then, in a blender, blitz the stir-fried onion, garlic and parsley with the nutmeg and stock.

3. Stir-fry the chicken livers and sweetbreads in the same large pot, adding a little oil if you need. Add the bay leaves, pepper, turmeric, oregano and the blender mix.

4. Cook on a medium heat for 20 minutes. If it dries, lower the heat and add a little more water.

5. Incorporate the previously washed and drained rice and add 1l (4 cups) of water.

6. Add salt and maintain a low heat so that the rice does not burn.

7. When the rice is cooked, garnish with some chopped parsley.

TINH

Teeny-tiny Tinh. Probably the smallest and most smiley of all the grandmothers we have cooked with and certainly the only granny covered in tattoos and wearing black Nike slides.

We found Tinh through her lovely daughter who runs Hanoi Cafe in London. When we met at her home, Tinh had her special Vietnamese knife in hand at all times. Watching her nip little pieces of carrot for the dipping sauce was highly satisfying. She prepared the rice paper and rolled the spring rolls with matching precision. After a few demonstrations we set up either side of her, wetting the rice paper until sticky and malleable enough to wrap the filling. Soon a large pile had formed and Tinh began the cooking process; straight into the hot oil to puff and crisp.

We ate from little bowls with noodles, salad and sauce, cutting the spring rolls in half with scissors for ease of eating. About seven spring rolls (each) and several hugs later, we left, Tinh blowing kisses in the doorway.

Born: *Hanoi, Vietnam, 1948*
Mother tongue: *Vietnamese*
Grandchildren: *Joseph, James, Calypso, Alfred, Edward*
They call her: *Ba Tinh*

This dish is eaten in Hanoi, where I'm from, as street food. My mother taught me how to make it, and it has become ever-present on the family menu. I even did it for my children's packed lunches at school. The key is to use all the coriander, including the stalks, because they hold the most flavour.

In the 1980s, thanks to political unrest in Vietnam, I was forced to flee from my home in Hanoi. My husband was Chinese and there was conflict between Vietnam and China at the time. We may well have been subject to ethnic cleansing if we had stayed. So we became part of the boat people migration that happened across the late 1970s and early 80s.

I sold all of my possessions in the hope I'd land in a better country, and boarded a boat I did not know the destination of. I had my two girls with me – just babies at the time – and my mother. I was only in my 30s and had to leave my husband behind, as he'd been imprisoned for being a part of a political group that angered the Vietnamese authorities.

The boats were tiny and there were so many people crammed into each one. They were basic fishing boats, so quite unsafe for the number of people trying to escape. I had to pack supplies for us all and had no idea how long we'd be on that boat for. My youngest daughter had dysentery and there was really nothing I could do; I felt so helpless. We were better off than others, though. Many didn't make the journey. I was witness to corpses being pushed off the boat. Then there was the fear of being robbed or raped by pirates, which we knew was a risk. We were on that boat for a month, floating along to nowhere.

By the time we were found, it was such a relief. We were discovered in the South China Sea by the Hong Kong authorities and were in a refugee camp in Hong Kong for a year. We were granted refugee status and stayed for around two years before we relocated to the UK. We had to share a bunk bed as a family of four. Still, it was better than that little boat in the middle of the sea.

I was so frightened for our safety in Vietnam that this was the only option for me and my family. The future was so uncertain that I could only see one way of securing it and that was to get out. That's really the only reason people have to put themselves through it. No other wordly options.

Fourteen years passed before my husband was released and finally joined the rest of the family in the UK. So much time had gone by that things weren't the same any more. I had become the matriarch of this all-female household and there was no room for a man any longer. My daughters couldn't even call him 'Dad'. So eventually we separated.

He was conservative and so different from who I had become. Part of me honouring my new self without him were these tattoos. I got my first one when I was 60. My first tattoo was an enormous one on my back. Since then I've had sleeves down both arms and legs. It was an affirmation that, 'You know what? This is who I am.' Every tattoo I have symbolises how I was feeling at the time. It's an expression of my entire life. These tattoos make me really very happy. I'm more myself now, in my old age, definitely.

—

Ba Tinh

BA TINH'S VIETNAMESE PORK AND CRAB SPRING ROLLS AND PICKLE SALAD

MEAT

FOR THE SALAD
(*Feeds 4-6*)

— 1 kohlrabi, peeled and julienned
— 2 large carrots (or 4 small),
   peeled and julienned
— stalks from 1 bunch fresh
   coriander, chopped into
   2.5cm (1in) pieces
— 1 tbsp granulated sugar
— 1 tsp sea salt
— 3 tbsp rice vinegar

FOR THE
SPRING ROLLS

— 250g (9oz) lean pork mince
— 100g (3½oz) crabmeat (one
   small tin)
— 2 small onions, finely diced
— ½ kohlrabi, peeled and finely diced
— 1 large carrot (or 2 small),
   peeled and finely diced
— 1 tsp granulated sugar
— 1 tsp salt
— 1 tbsp fish sauce
— 1 egg, beaten
— 3 tbsp rice vinegar
— 1 x 12-pack rice spring roll
   wrappers (22cm/9in diameter)
— vegetable oil, for frying

FOR THE DIPPING
WATER (*nuoc cham*)

— 1 tbsp granulated sugar
— 1 small carrot, cut into very fine
   pieces (Tinh takes slivers from
   the top, moving around to create
   pretty, tiny pieces)
— 2 garlic cloves, very finely sliced
— 3 tbsp rice vinegar
— red bird's-eye chillies, very finely
   sliced (to taste)

METHOD

1. For the salad: prepare the kohlrabi and carrots and put them into a bowl.

2. Take the coriander stalks and add to the vegetables, saving the leaves for another dish. (Tinh says most of the flavour is in the stalks!)

3. Add the sugar, salt and vinegar and mix well. Place into the fridge until needed.

4. For the spring rolls: in a bowl, mix the pork and crab. Add the diced onions, kohlrabi and carrot, followed by the sugar, salt, fish sauce and egg. Stir until well combined.

5. Next, get the wrappers ready by preparing a small bowl of just-boiled water with the rice vinegar. Have the wrappers to hand and prepare one at a time on a board or plate.

6. Dip your hand into the water and stroke the water all over both sides of the rice wrapper, until it's transparent and becoming loose and sticky.

7. On the side of the wrapper closest to you, put a heaped tablespoon of pork filling. Roll the closest edge over, tuck tightly and roll to the middle. Bring the sides in and roll up until secure. Place on a clean, dampened tea towel or greased tray so they aren't touching, otherwise they might stick together.

8. Repeat until all the rolls are done. Then heat 1cm (½in) vegetable oil in a flat-bottomed pan – you're shallow frying, not deep-frying. Make sure the oil is nice and hot before putting your rolls in. Work in batches, so they don't stick together and fry for 8 minutes, or until lightly browned and crisp. Keep the finished rolls in a warm place until ready to serve.

9. For the dipping water: in a heatproof jug or bowl, dissolve the sugar in a touch of boiling water. Tip the carrot and garlic slivers in and add the rice vinegar. Add the chilli last, taste and adjust the sweet-sour ratio to your taste by adding more vinegar or sugar, as you like. Don't be tempted to skip this sauce – it really makes the dish.

10. Serve the crispy spring rolls with the dipping sauce, salad and vermicelli noodles.

Tip: If you want to make a veggie version of the spring rolls, substitute the pork and crab for mushrooms or crumbled firm tofu.

Grandmother Hsu Chen Xiu's Taiwanese Stir-Fry Vermicelli (*Chao Mi Fen*)

Erchen Chang, chef

Ingredients

— 150g (6oz) pork belly
— 4cm (1½in) of ginger, sliced
— 1 spring onion
— 1 tbsp Shaoxing wine
— 250g (9oz) thin rice vermicelli
— 2–3 Thai shallots, thinly sliced
— 30g (1oz) dried shrimp
— 50g (1¾oz) dried shiitake mushrooms, rehydrated and sliced
— 2–3 tbsp pork lard
— 2–3 tbsp soy sauce
— 1 tsp mirin
— 50g (1¾oz) carrot, julienned
— 250g (9oz) flat cabbage, sliced
— 30g (1oz) celery sticks, finely chopped
— bunch fresh coriander

My grandmother's name is Hsu Chen Xiu, which translates to 'Beauty of the Chen family'. She is the kindest, toughest lady I know. She became a mother figure at the age of six, raising her younger brother. She grew up in Taipei, but after marrying my grandfather she moved to the south of Taiwan. There she had seven beautiful children of her own and has always been a helping hand to so many.

Growing up, my most vivid memory is her cycling on her red bike, the front basket full of food from the market, vegetables sticking out in every direction and both handles heavy with bags of poached goose (my grandfather's favourite).

This stir-fry – *Chao Mi Fen* – is my grandmother's signature dish. It's served at every occasion, from Chinese New Year to high-school graduation and even for the neighbour's son's wedding. Every time I am back in Taiwan, my grandmother welcomes me home with a large bowl. The flavours are simple yet complex. There are a few things you must do: you have to use the best dried shiitake mushrooms, find a rice vermicelli that is made from 100 per cent rice, get sweet flat cabbage and most importantly, you must cook the dish with pork lard for that extra Taiwanese flavour.

Feeds 4

1. Place the pork belly into a pan of boiling water. Once the water is brought back to boiling point, switch off the heat and discard the water.

2. Cover the blanched pork belly with cold water; add a couple of slices of ginger, the spring onion and a dash of Shaoxing wine. Bring to the boil then turn the heat down to medium–low. The water should be at a low simmer. Let it poach for 30 minutes, switch off the heat and let it rest for another 15 minutes with a lid on.

3. Take the pork belly out of the water (keep the poaching liquid aside for later use), cover with cling film and let it cool down completely.

4. Once the pork belly has cooled down, slice the belly into 3mm (⅛in)-thick slices.

5. Soak the rice vermicelli in cold water.

6. In a wok, fry the sliced shallots, dried shrimp, shiitake slices and sliced poached pork with pork lard on a high heat. Stir-fry until golden and fragrant and then add the soy, mirin and carrot to the wok and let the flavours settle for a couple of minutes.

7. Take most of the ingredients out of the wok, leaving some cooked pork slices in. Add a bit more lard and stir-fry the cabbage until cooked.

8. Drain the vermicelli and add to the wok with a bit of the pork belly poaching liquid then season with soy and add the rest of the stir-fried ingredients back in.

9. Serve and garnish with finely chopped celery and fresh coriander.

MARGIT

Iska's grandmother, 'Lally', is a slight lady now and much less adept at getting around than she once was. She wears thick glasses and struggles to make out shapes. Still, her dress sense is impeccable and she has an air of refinement about her that can be quite intimidating (much like Iska), regardless of her age.

She may well have been born in Germany to German parents but not a trace of her heritage remains in her accent. A clipped received-pronunciation English betrays nothing of her past, which spilled out over a weekend spent sipping tea and chopping 'granny carrots' with her in her bright, modernist-feeling Exeter home in the UK.

While Iska and our photographer, Ella, fiddled with food styling in the kitchen (you don't want to know what happened to that beer to keep it fizzy for the photo), Lally and I took to the living room for a brew.

I couldn't have prepared for the emotion that our chat would solicit from me. It wasn't the Nazi stories, the nostalgia over a first boyfriend, or the cruelty she faced after fleeing Germany that led to my locking myself in the bathroom and bursting into tears. It was the way she described the loss of the husband she had held so dear and the moment she walked into the room to hear the nurse say his heart had stopped beating. 'That was like an explosion,' she told me, and my own heart felt an aftershock from that impact.

—

Anastasia on Iska's Granny

Born: *Lichtenfels, Germany, 1928*
Mother tongue: *German*
Grandchildren: *Iska, Luke, Harry, Jack, Rosie, Coco, Francesca*
They call her: *Lally*

Schnitzel is a German favourite of mine, but for a long time after moving to England I was very set on not being German. When I went walking through town with my mum, I'd always try and stop her talking so noisily. She'd let the cat out of the bag of course and people would know we were foreign. People used to ask me if I knew Hitler. We'd then have to explain why we were 'good' Germans. We really weren't welcome anywhere. In Germany we were persecuted by the Nazis. They poisoned my pet dog and impaled artwork by expressionist painter friends of my parents on the railings of my father's factory.

I'd walk to school from my house every day, but on one occasion my mum arrived in the car to say we were going on holiday. I was so surprised to see her picking me up in the car. She'd never done that before, and I was confused because I didn't even have my holiday clothes with me. She drove straight from school to the nearest airport, parked the car, left the key in it and then booked a flight, which we boarded that afternoon. I never learned exactly what sparked that decision for her to leave on that day in particular, but I know it saved our lives.

I didn't eat or cook any German food until I was well into my 20s. The meat part of the schnitzel is my favourite part, but trying to find a good vegetable accompaniment is sometimes hard because the dish itself is so dry. I was once invited to dinner by an Austrian lady who thought she knew everything about food, and she told me to really enjoy a schnitzel properly, you just have a nicely dressed salad with it. She didn't even have any potatoes with hers. I thought it was very odd, no carbohydrates.

As fate would have it, my first boyfriend was a German man. I met him when I was a student at the Royal College of Music in London. He first pursued me up the stairs going to the canteen. He looked at my tray and I had my baked beans on toast on there and he said, 'Do you like this food?' and I said, 'Well, I hope I shall.' We got to talking and he realised I was very much the same as him. We decided to go out for a meal at some cheap little place in Soho that evening and so it went on. It was a rather good night. That was quite a good time in life, really.

I met my husband Michael around the same time and all our first outings were food-orientated. I never thought about marriage and I was always ready to say 'no', but marrying Michael was the right decision when it happened in 1954. We were in some pub in Leicester when he proposed. One day he said, 'D'you think we'd better get on with it?' It's the sort of thing Michael would say, instead of falling on one knee and doing all that stuff.

I can just remember one meal we had in Colwyn Bay, when Michael's medical partner and his wife were coming for dinner and they came a little bit too early. I was doing duck. Why I should want to do duck, I don't know. I dropped it on the kitchen floor. I was going to baste it, I think. Anyway, I promptly scooped it up, put it back in its tray and popped it back into the oven. No one knew. I told Michael afterwards.

He was lovely and very matter-of-fact about things that you could have been rightfully hysterical about and that's what made it such a happy marriage - his tremendous readiness to compromise. If I could have anyone over for dinner, it would be him again. Michael and my children.

—

Lally Margit

LALLY MARGIT'S GERMAN SCHNITZEL, RED CABBAGE AND 'GRANNY CARROTS'

FOR THE SCHNITZEL
(Feeds 4–6)

— 4 pork leg escalopes
— 2 tbsp plain flour
— 1 egg, beaten
— 6 tbsp white breadcrumbs
— 100g (7 tbsp) butter

FOR THE RED CABBAGE

— 100g (7 tbsp) butter
— ½ onion, finely sliced
  into half-moons
— 1 red cabbage, quartered,
  with heart removed and
  leaves finely shredded
— ½ cooking apple, grated
— 2 garlic cloves, finely sliced
— ½ nutmeg, grated
— 3 tbsp balsamic vinegar
— 3 tbsp white wine vinegar
— 1 tsp brown sugar
— 5g (small handful)
  whole juniper berries
— juice of ½ a lemon

FOR THE GRANNY CARROTS

— 150g (⅔ cup) butter
— ½ onion, diced
— 6 carrots, peeled and cut into
  small 0.5cm (¼in) squares
— 1 tbsp granulated sugar
— juice of ½ a lemon
— handful fresh parsley,
  finely chopped

SCHNITZEL

1. Blot the pork with kitchen towel to ensure it's dry.

2. Use a meat mallet or rolling pin to bash the meat all over on both sides to flatten. It should be around 1cm (½in) thick, or less.

3. Prepare three plates: the first with flour, the second with beaten egg and the third with breadcrumbs. Season the breadcrumbs with sea salt and freshly ground black pepper.

4. Get a spare dish ready and begin to pass each of the escalopes through the flour, egg and breadcrumbs, making a finished pile on the plate.

5. Melt a knob of butter in a large frying pan and sizzle the schnitzels for 3–4 minutes on each side, or until golden brown and cooked through. You may need to do these in batches; if so, keep the finished schnitzel warm until ready to serve.

RED CABBAGE

1. Put the butter into a pan on medium heat to melt. Add the onion and soften (around 10 minutes).

2. Next, add all the red cabbage and carefully stir to coat in the butter.

3. Add all the other ingredients, season, stir and leave to cook on a low–medium heat with the lid on for 40–50 minutes, until soft.

4. Stir every so often to ensure the cabbage doesn't burn on the bottom of the pan. Taste and adjust seasoning, if needed, before serving.

GRANNY CARROTS

1. Gently melt the butter in a pan and cook the onion for around 10 minutes, until nice and soft.

2. Add the carrots, sugar and lemon juice, plus salt and pepper, stirring to coat.

3. Cook on a medium heat with the lid on for 15 minutes, or until the carrots have softened but still have a little bite to them. Stir in the parsley and serve.

Hotpot Mabel's Yorkshire Lamb Hotpot

Kathy Slack, food writer and supper-club host

Ingredients

— 75g (5 tbsp) dripping (or butter if you can't get dripping)
— 1kg (2¼lb) lamb shoulder, cut into 5cm (2in) chunks
— 1 large onion, sliced
— 2 sticks celery, chopped into 2cm (¾in) chunks
— 6 carrots, peeled and chopped into 2cm (¾in) chunks
— 3 bay leaves
— 20g (2 tbsp) plain flour
— 600ml (2½ cups) lamb stock (or an Oxo cube in 600ml/2½ cups of water if you want to be very traditional)
— 1 tbsp Henderson's Relish (a Sheffield brand; use Worcestershire sauce if you can't find it)
— 1kg (2¼lb) old potatoes, peeled and cut into 0.5cm (¼in) slices
— 50g (4 tbsp) butter, cut into small chunks

My grandmother was known to us all as 'Hotpot'. In fact, until I was eight or nine, I thought hotpot was the generic name for all grandmothers – grans, grandmas, grannies, hotpots. She was so called because of her legendary lamb hotpot.

Her hotpot expertise was especially notable for two reasons. First, she was a good Yorkshire woman, so her skill at making lamb hotpot, traditionally a Lancashire dish, a county for which the Yorkshire folk hold an ancient grudge, was practically heretical. And second, because she was, in all other respects, a really terrible cook: soggy sprouts, lumpy mash, grey beef topside that went in the oven the day before you arrived. But when it came to the hotpot, she was unsurpassed.

This is, mostly, her recipe. She didn't brown her meat or sweat her vegetables or anything so fancy; she just slung it all in the pot: 'Nowt a couple of hours and a lump of Oxo won't fix'. I do both of those things, though I'm sure she would consider it wildly ostentatious.

Feeds 4-6

1. Melt half of the dripping in a large casserole dish over a medium–high heat. Season the meat and fry it in the dripping until browned. This is best done in batches to avoid overcrowding the pan, which prevents the meat from browning.

2. Once all the lamb is browned and removed from the casserole dish, add the rest of the dripping and turn the heat down a touch. Tip in the onion, celery, carrots, bay leaves and a pinch of salt and sweat gently for 10–15 minutes until the vegetables are soft.

3. Sprinkle the flour over the vegetables and cook for 3–4 minutes, stirring as you go. This will stop the dish tasting powdery.

4. Preheat oven to 150°C/130°C fan/300°F/gas 2.

5. Return the meat to the dish and pour over the stock and the Henderson's Relish. You want the liquid to just cover the meat, so add a splash of water if you need to. Bring to the boil then turn the hob off.

6. Arrange the sliced potatoes on top of the stew in layers then dot the pieces of butter amongst the potatoes and sprinkle with a pinch of salt.

7. Put a lid on the casserole dish and bake in the oven for 2 hours.

8. Just before you are ready to serve, turn the oven up to 220°C/200°C fan/ 425°F/gas 7, take the lid off the dish and cook for a further 10 minutes to brown the potatoes. Serve bubbling hot to a crowded table full of expectant grandchildren.

MARAL

Jet-lagged but wide-eyed at all there was to take in in New York, we hopped on the subway from Manhattan to Brooklyn to be welcomed into a small apartment by a lady with a big heart. She swung open the door to her home and exclaimed, 'What beautiful girls,' before demanding we glug tea (foraged herbs from her native mountain home, including wild mint and dried roses) and guzzle down a lavash she'd just whipped up.

The lavash, a sort of bread pocket filled with herbed meat, which resembles a flattened calzone, is what Maral describes as a 'snack' – but we were full after sharing just one. While we ate, she moved. She danced around her teeny kitchen for four hours, chopping up, whizzing up, rubbing in, marinating, bubbling and stirring until we were seated at a table laden with far too much food for three.

We ate: lamb *dolma*, which Maral got us to prepare, sticking our tentative hands into a great bowl of meat, chopped onions and herbs, before we extracted small balls of it to wrap in wet vine leaves. Also on the menu were peppers and tomatoes stuffed with lamb and fresh bread, rolled and griddled just moments before we dined. This was all swilled down with vodka, the climax of our afternoon being an Azerbaijani dance-off in the living room. Hours later, we escaped into the cool winter air of Brooklyn, our cheeks flushed and our hearts as full as our stomachs.

'Don't stay in a hotel and spend your money; next time, you stay with me,' she said, waving us off.

Born: *Azerbaijan, 1958*
Mother tongue: *Persian*
Grandchildren: *Olivia, Megan, Adrianna*
They call her: *Baba*

I'm from a family where every member of my family knows how to cook the entire animal from head to tail. It's so important not to waste when it comes to food. We're from the mountains in Azerbaijan. It's so beautiful there that you can hear the voice of the river as you sleep. Mostly we grew our own vegetables and had cows, sheep, chickens. It's so different now, though – it's become a ski resort and a place for tourists.

I collect all my tea from Azerbaijan when I go home for four months in the summer. When I was a little girl, my mum would take us into the forest and mountains and she would show us which herbs to pick so we

could forage ourselves for all of our teas. I now bring so much back with me from Azerbaijan. I don't even know the name of some of the herbs I bring back with me. It's so important to have the ingredients I know and love from my home.

When I was in Azerbaijan I worked as a midwife, and then a nurse in Siberia, then I became a derma-tologist. I married and had two children, but my husband left me for a young Russian student. That's when I took my two young daughters and moved to America to start from zero at the age of 41. I did any job available - cleaning peoples' apartments. Anything. Then I finished college here.

My husband came back after 20 years to ask for forgiveness. I told him, 'I forgive you, but I don't need you.' The truth is I never loved him and I think that's what pushed him away. I don't know how I lived with him for 14 years, to be honest.

If you're not scared and have a goal inside you, you can do anything anywhere. You just need to go straight on and never look back. I didn't speak a single word of English when I came here. I never had any idea that I would be living in Brooklyn in New York City and that I would need to speak English. I learned within five months, though. I had a technique, which was to speak to everyone.

When I took the train I would speak to the person next to me and ask them, 'Speak English with me?' I would say, 'Please you tell me if I say wrong,' and they would, so that is how I learned. From Washington Heights for an hour and a half to my home, I would talk to everyone. Can you believe? I had the same conversation a hundred times. If you want to talk, you have to talk with people. You're not supposed to be shy. If you want to learn a language it is no use doing the book thing.

I'm fast; I always want to learn. I attended college along with my daughter and studied biochemistry. I just don't stop, ever. I'm always moving and doing things. You told me 'cook one recipe' today and I'm making six dishes. It's just something in me. I like to keep busy.

I love to cook. I always have guests over to share my dinner table with. My mother and father always had people over too. If you came to my father's house, we would have a huge table for 40 people. The men would prepare the sheep for the slaughter and the women would be cooking.

—

Baba Maral

BABA MARAL'S AZERBAIJANI
STUFFED VINE LEAVES (*Dolma*)

INGREDIENTS
(*Feeds 4-6*)

— 250g (9oz) lamb mince
— 250g (9oz) beef mince
— 1 medium onion,
  finely chopped
— 1 small potato, finely diced
— 2 tbsp fresh dill, chopped
— 2 tbsp fresh coriander,
  chopped
— 1 tsp paprika
— 30-ish vine leaves
— ½ quince or one small
  apple, roughly chopped
— 2 garlic cloves, peeled

METHOD

1. Place the meat, onion, potato, herbs and paprika in a bowl.
   Season and combine with your hands.

2. Take your vine leaves one by one and put a small ball of meat mixture
   in the bottom part of the leaf. Then, starting from the right-hand side
   and working round, fold the leaf in on itself until it covers the meat.

3. Place the finished stuffed leaves into a saucepan as you go, packing
   them so the leaf is secure and won't unwrap.

4. When they're all done, place the quince or apple pieces and garlic
   on top. Add cold water halfway up the saucepan and turn the heat
   up high until it comes to the boil. Then lower the heat to a simmer
   and cook for 30–40 minutes, until cooked through.

BABA MARAL'S AZERBAIJANI STUFFED AUBERGINES, PEPPERS AND TOMATOES (*'Three Sisters'*)

INGREDIENTS
(*Feeds 4-6*)

— 120g (heaped ½ cup)
  white rice
— 500g (1lb) lamb mince
— 1 tbsp olive oil
— 1 white onion, finely diced
— 1 red onion, finely diced
— 1 large handful fresh dill,
  chopped
— 1 large handful fresh
  coriander, chopped
— 1 tbsp dried mint
— 1 tbsp dried oregano
— 1 tbsp dried mountain
  mint (optional)
— 1 tsp salt
— 1 tsp cracked black pepper
— 1 tsp paprika
— 2 red and 2 yellow peppers
— 4 large tomatoes
— 5 mini aubergines
— 1 apple or ½ a quince,
  chopped
— 3 garlic cloves,
  finely chopped

METHOD

1. Cook the rice until al dente, about 5 minutes. You don't want it cooked all the way through, as it will have baking time inside the vegetables as well.

2. Meanwhile, start browning the lamb in a non-stick pan with the olive oil, breaking it up with a wooden spoon as you go. When the meat is browned all over and the rice is al dente, set both aside to cool a little.

3. Once cool enough to touch, use your hands to combine the meat and rice with the onions, herbs, salt, black pepper and paprika.

4. Partially slice the tops off the peppers but don't slice all the way through, to create a lid that hinges open, through which you can take out all the insides. Do the same for the tomatoes, trying to keep the lid attached and taking out the middle (reserve this for later).

5. Slice the tops off the aubergines and make a slice lengthways with a little gap at each end to create a pocket ready for filling.

6. Stuff all your veg carefully with the lamb mixture – the lids should still close with a little space for the mixture to expand further. Place the veg in a large casserole pan with a lid so they're upright and holding each other up. Top with the quince or apple, garlic and tomato middles.

7. Turn the hob to medium-low and cook the pan of stuffed veg for 20 minutes with the lid on (and no added water!). Be careful not to overdo them, you want them to keep their shape! Serve with olives, rice and flatbreads.

TOOTSIE

Having found her number through the famous barbecue smokehouse she works for in Texas, after weeks of trying to get hold of her, we called Tootsie, huddled around a phone we'd put on loudspeaker. The line was not at all great. 'Hello?' barked a gruff voice, more demanding than enquiring. We dived into explaining that we're two British girls on a mission to share recipes from grandmothers all over the wo— 'WHO may I ASK is SPEAKING?' the voice bellowed in a thick Texan slur. A quick exchange of glances. Then we tried again.

Eventually, over a painful five minutes and excruciatingly temperamental phone line, we were told to go to Snow's BBQ in Lexington from 5 a.m. on a Saturday. Any Saturday? She had already hung up. So, weeks later, as we drove through lush fields dotted with cattle to small-town Lexington, we were perhaps more nervous than we have ever been when meeting a grandmother for the first time.

We needn't have worried. Tootsie had been up since 2 a.m. smoking brisket over hot coals. Snow's BBQ is famous all over the USA and octogenarian pitmaster Tootsie is its biggest draw. Hundreds of people drive from all over Texas to try her brisket. At Snow's, she's a celebrity, constantly in demand and forever being photographed by fans. In spite of all of this, she still gave us her full attention, sharing her prime brisket with us, taking us through her favourite beef stew recipe and opening up so honestly about her life, the death of her husband, and how her love of work will keep her going for years to come. Her bark, it seems, was much worse than her bite.

Born: *Lexington, Texas, USA, 1935*
Mother tongue: *American English*
Grandchildren: *Nathan, Crystal, Ashley, Casera, Cody, Seth, Alaya, Alison, Harley, Peyton, Whiatt, Zoe, Cody Jr, Savannah*
They call her: *Mamaw*

The recipes I use are hand-me-down recipes, I guess. It's stuff passed on to me from people I've worked with. My husband loved beef stew. It was something he would like if I cooked it all day and the meat would just fall apart. We're big beef people in Texas. When I was caring for my husband, I'd have to take him to see his cattle every day. Oh boy, he loved his cattle.

My husband and I ran our own meat market for 20 years. He then suffered a stroke and was unable to move around. I had to quit to take care of him. For a month or so, he was even blind. When he was in the hospital, we didn't even realise.

Then one day he said, 'I can't see anything out there,' and I realised he'd lost his sight.

I was caring for him for five years before he went to the nursing home. It's very hard. My husband was 6 feet tall, 200lbs and I'm 5 feet 3. I was having to lift him to take him to the bathroom in the middle of the night. It was a lot of tugging. We'd fallen a few times together. It was tough. I sometimes had to call the police to come and help, because if you call an ambulance in Texas, they have to take you to the hospital.

Losing him and my son three months apart was the hardest

thing, but I have so many people around me to help me through. I have my barbecue family. It's funny to think I came at the whole barbecuing world by accident. Many years ago, when I was a stay-at-home mom to three children, someone didn't show up at my husband's work one day, so he asked if I'd come and help out with the barbecue pit. I said, 'I'll do the best I can. I've never done anything like that, but I'll try.'

That was 1966. Now I'm a pitmaster and people drive here from all over Texas for my barbecue brisket. I put my briskets on, on Saturday morning at 2 a.m. in order for them to be ready at 8.30 a.m. for people arriving for a feed. By 11 a.m., everything's gone.

The food world sure has changed a lot in my lifetime. Box beef was only just coming into the rural area when I first started working in food. We just had hanging meat. Then in the 90s we started to get specific cuts of meat in a box, which was much more industrialised. The meats I had learned to cut up and work with were from an entire animal. I was doing the butchering and slaughtering, but that never bothered me. I was raised on a farm and we butchered our own hogs in the winter time and in the spring we'd butcher chickens. If you're going to eat meat, you need to know where it's coming from.

I can't understand why younger generations don't eat certain parts of the animal. I was brought up in the Depression and we were told either you eat this or you don't eat. You ate it and you were thankful you had food on the table. It upsets me when kids say, 'I don't like that,' and have never even tried it.

It's so important in life to be happy with what you have. Our purpose in life is to make the very best of what we have. I'm trying to do that every day.
—
Mamaw Tootsie

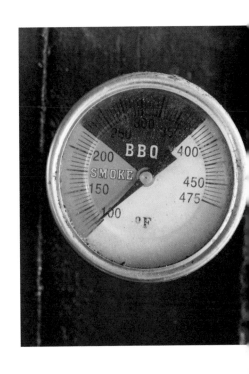

MAMAW TOOTSIE'S BEEF STEW

INGREDIENTS
(Feeds 4)

— 3 tbsp olive oil
— 2 large red onions,
  each cut into 8 wedges
— 3 carrots, peeled,
  halved lengthways and
  cut into 2cm (¾in) pieces
— 3 red potatoes, peeled
  and roughly chopped
  into 2cm (¾in) cubes
— 3 tbsp plain flour
— 2 tsp salt flakes
— 2 tsp cracked black pepper
— 700g (1½lb) braising beef,
  diced
— 4 sprigs fresh thyme
— 1l (4 cups) beef stock
— handful fresh parsley,
  chopped (for garnish)

METHOD

1. In a heavy casserole pan, heat 2 tbsp of the olive oil and fry the onions for 10 minutes until starting to brown.

2. Add the carrots and potatoes, and cook for 5–10 minutes until colouring a little.

3. Meanwhile, mix the flour, salt and pepper together. Sprinkle over the beef cubes and toss so they're lightly coated.

4. When the vegetables look slightly caramelised at the edges, remove them from the pan and set aside. Add the remaining tbsp olive oil.

5. Brown the beef in 2 batches, making sure it gets some good colour on all sides.

6. Return all the beef and all the vegetables to the pan; add the thyme and stock.

7. Bring to the boil and then simmer with the lid on for 2½ hours, or until the beef is falling apart.

8. Remove the lid and cook uncovered for the last 20–30 minutes so the sauce thickens. Season to taste and serve with crusty bread and a sprinkle of parsley.

Mam Gwladys's Seeded Yorkshire Puddings

Anna Jones, cook and food writer

Ingredients

- 200g (1½ cups) plain white flour
- 2 tbsp toasted poppy seeds
- 2 tbsp toasted sesame seeds
- 1 tsp sea salt
- pinch cracked black pepper
- 250ml (1 cup + 1 tbsp) milk, topped up to 300ml (1¼ cups) with water
- 4 organic or free-range eggs
- 12 tsp rapeseed oil or groundnut oil

One of the things we British do best is a Sunday dinner. Mine have and always will focus around one thing – the Yorkshire pudding. I am from a really big family – my dad is number 9 of 12 children. I have 30 cousins, a brother and a sister. So Sunday dinners at my nan's were quite something. Dinner was in shifts, and as the littlest we always got to go first, which filled my heart with joy because it was a guarantee of one of Mam's Yorkshires (which I am still sure are the best I've ever had).

So here, aged six, the obsession started. I have tried every Yorkshire recipe that's going but I like my Yorkshires to have a bit of stodge – crispy and light on the outside, doughy chewiness on the inside. I have added some toasted seeds here for texture and flavour, which lifts this from an add-on to the main event.

There are five commandments of Yorkshire puddings. Don't be scared of heat: preheat your oven to maximum. Try to rest your batter for at least 15 minutes. It's key. Be sure to preheat your oil in the oven until smoking hot. Make sure you heat the tray on the hob while pouring in your batter. Don't open the door until the cooking time is up or the Yorkshires will deflate. Finally, rapeseed oil works well here – it's a brilliant British oil whose vivid saffron hue paints the outside of the Yorkshires. Sunday heaven.

Makes 12 towering Yorkshires

1. First preheat your oven to as hot as it will go. Next, mix the flour, toasted seeds, salt and pepper in a bowl. Pour your milk-water mix into a jug.

2. Crack the eggs into the bowl of flour, pour in a little of the milk mixture, and beat well until you have got rid of most of the lumps. Continue to beat in the rest of the milk mixture bit by bit, until you have a smooth batter about the consistency of double cream. Now leave your batter to rest for at least 15 minutes.

3. Once your batter is ready, pour it into a jug. Put about 1 tsp of oil into each of the little dips in a 12-hole muffin tin and pop it into the oven for a couple of minutes, until the fat is smoking.

4. Now turn 2 of the rings on your hob to medium and put the jug of batter next to the hob. Very carefully but quickly, take the hot muffin tin out of the oven and shut the door. Put the muffin tray on the heat and quickly but carefully pour the batter into each hole until it is about 2cm (¾in) from the top.

5. Put the tray back into the oven, shut the door and set the timer for 12 minutes. Do not be tempted to open the door too soon – they WILL fall and fail. Check through the oven glass at 12 minutes and if they are risen like little towers and nicely golden, take them out. If not, leave them in without opening the oven for another few minutes, keeping an eye on them.

JUNE

June ran the picture framer's at the end of Broadway Market in Hackney, London. You'd go to drop off a picture and discuss framing options (she had a very good eye) and end up staying for 40 minutes, gossiping about the man upstairs and receiving a step-by-step account of her recent holiday to Japan. The only way to leave was to slowly edge out of the door until you could make a run for it, or if someone else arrived to take your place.

It was a laugh a minute at June's from the moment she met us at the door, wearing bright white Nike running shoes with fluorescent pink laces. It was November, and cold with crisp sunlight coming through the vertical blinds into her open-plan kitchen. A well-stocked drinks trolley stood next to the plastic pram of her granddaughter's dolly. There were dolls and teddies in most corners.

Most grannies cook and recall stories in tandem. June liked to stop all cooking and use her entire body and every facial muscle to tell her stories. This meant the food took a very long time to prepare, but the tales and performances were top quality. We had the pie with super-creamy dauphinoise potatoes, 'posh' heritage carrots and lots of gravy.

June is the only grandmother who is no longer with us as we write. Perhaps she was ill when we cooked together, but we never would have guessed. She was totally exuberant from start to finish. How lucky we are to have spent that time with her, capturing her zest for life and her recipe.

Born: *London, UK, 1948*
Mother tongue: *English*
Grandchild: *Marloe, Jude*
They call her: *Nanny*

Bobby, my son-in-law, is always asking me to make him a pie. I've had strict instructions not to make him any more though, because of the weight issue. I've been making this as far back as I can remember. I don't actually remember not making it, but it is a bit of an east London dish.

The area's been home for so many years now. We lived in Stepney Green when I was a girl and I went to a Jewish school. I actually used to swim for the Stepney Jewish Girls' Club. I don't know how that happened, because I'm not Jewish. I even learned Hebrew.

East London has changed so much, though. Broadway Market is disgusting. Gentrification has gone over the top. The locals are all being pushed out and all of a sudden these blocks are becoming 'luxury' areas and no one is stopping it. There's been a 100 per cent price increase on my building now. I've no idea where my framing business is going to go. I'm completely blank. It's such a self-destructive thing that's happening to London. It isn't sustainable. It's so sad.

I've been a framer for 25 years now. Before that I had my own recruitment firm. I hadn't had any training. I just worked as an interviewer for an employment agency and one day I thought to myself, 'I can do this.' I had so many contacts, so I took them all with me. Then, when I had the recruitment firm, I saw the guy next to my office had a framing shop. It was so, so different to what I was doing behind a desk. So I learned everything there was to know about framing from scratch and then took over his business.

Oh, and I had a gallery in Belgium at one point too. I've crammed so much into this life of mine by doing things! I used to go backwards and forwards with a group of girls to Ostend, this mad clubbing area. It was wild there. I was once in Lille and I was so drunk (I don't know how I ended up there). There was a puddle and I remember walking through the water with my high heels on, absolutely drunk. That's a memory of getting my feet wet. I don't think I've ever done that since.

I was pretty wild. Another time I was in a bar in Ostend and I said to somebody, 'Where's the ladies' here?' They pointed it out, I went on through and saw a ladder. So I climbed it. I went up this ladder right up into the loft. They'd sent me up there as a joke.

It was one of these weekends that I saw the gallery in Belgium was for rent with an apartment upstairs. I thought it might be fun, so I took it on. I'd drive from London to Dover on a Friday night after work with all this art in my little maroon Mini, get on the boat and arrive in Belgium, where all the clubs would be. So of course, I'd go out at about 1 a.m.

I do think it's funny, as you get older you go out, meet up with the girls, do a little ladies-who-lunch thing, but I do realise, all we talk about is the things we used to do. It's all hilarious, you know, like the time we lost Joan in Paris or whatever, but after you've done it two or three times, you think, What about now? What are we doing now?
—

Nanny June

NANNY JUNE'S DAUPHINOISE POTATOES

INGREDIENTS
(*Feeds 6*)

— 400ml (1⅔ cups) semi-skimmed milk
— 200ml (scant 1 cup) double cream
— 3 garlic cloves, crushed
— 3 sprigs fresh thyme, leaves picked
— 2 bay leaves
— 1kg (2¼lb) Maris Piper potatoes, peeled and thinly sliced (about 3mm/⅛in thick)
— 1 large onion, finely sliced into half-moons
— 40g (⅓ cup) Gruyère, grated
— 25g (2 tbsp) butter, plus extra for greasing
— nutmeg, grated

METHOD

1. Preheat oven to 200°C/180°C fan/ 400°F/gas 6. Pour the semi-skimmed milk and double cream into a big saucepan.

2. Add the garlic, thyme and bay leaves and bring to the boil. Remove from the heat and add the potatoes and onion. Return to the heat, bring to the boil and lower to a simmer for 3–5 minutes.

3. When the potatoes are tender, tip into a large greased ovenproof dish. Scatter with the grated Gruyère, dot with butter and sprinkle with nutmeg. Bake for 40 minutes, until golden brown on top.

NANNY JUNE'S
ENGLISH STEAK PIE

INGREDIENTS
(*Feeds 6*)

— 1kg (2¼lb) stewing beef, chopped into large chunks (shin and skirt are good, but if you're feeling really fancy, June insists rump steak is the best)
— 2 tbsp olive oil
— 2 large onions, chopped
— 2 garlic cloves, chopped
— 4 tbsp plain flour
— 5 bay leaves
— 1l (4 cups) beef stock
— 125ml (½ cup) red wine
— 1 x 500g (1lb) block shortcrust pastry

METHOD

1. In a large sauté pan, brown the onions and garlic in 1 tbsp oil.

2. Put the beef in a large bowl and sprinkle with the flour. Stir to coat.

3. Remove the onion mixture from the heat, transfer to a bowl and place the beef into the same pan with the remaining 1 tbsp oil. Brown the beef for 2 minutes, stirring, to seal in the flavours.

4. Add the onion mixture back into the pan along with the bay leaves. Pour in 1l (4 cups) hot beef stock and simmer gently for 3 hours with the lid on. Add the red wine and stew for a further 30 minutes (June says don't put this in any earlier as it could make the meat tough).

5. Grease and flour a 20cm (8in) pie dish and preheat oven to 200°C/180°C fan/ 400°F/gas 6.

6. Cut ⅓ off your block of pastry and set aside for the lid. Roll the remaining ⅔ out to a size that will easily line the dish with a little extra over the edge. Place gently into the dish, press lightly into the corners and fold the inside edges round and over the edge of the pie dish slightly.

7. Scoop out the pieces of beef with a slotted spoon (you don't want too much sauce in the pie), let cool a little and place into the pie dish – it should look nice and full and be slightly higher than the rim. Save the juices to serve as gravy with the pie.

8. Roll out the remaining pastry and place on top, pushing down to join it with the under layer. Cut away the excess and add fork lines around the edge. Decorate your pie as you like with the excess pastry. (June made a little 15cm/6in plait – why not?)

9. Bake for 45 minutes, until beautifully golden brown. Rest for 10 minutes before serving.

Grandma Pouran Heydari's Iranian Spiced Beef with Eggs and Spring Onions (*Vaavishkaa*)

Yasmin Khan, food and travel writer and broadcaster

Ingredients

— 450g (1lb) minced beef
— 1 medium onion, finely chopped
— 400ml (1¾ cups) water
— 1 tsp turmeric
— ½ tsp cracked black pepper
— 4 tomatoes
— 2 tbsp tomato purée
— ¼ tsp cayenne pepper
— 1 tsp sea salt
— 2 tbsp sunflower oil
— 2 eggs
— 2 spring onions, trimmed and finely chopped, to garnish

My maternal grandmother, Pouran Heydari, came from rural northern Iran. She was a determinedly strong and resourceful woman who sadly endured much trauma and tragedy in her life, often giving her a heavy air of sadness and melancholy that she carried with her everywhere. One of the things that did make her happy, though, was feeding her grandchildren, all of whom she treated with much love and affection. This was a meal she often cooked for us. It is called *vaavishkaa*, not a typical Iranian word but rather sounds as if it may be of Russian origin, which is unsurprising, given the trade activity along the shores of the Caspian Sea over the centuries. Whatever its origins, it is a great dish to make if you want to whip up something quick and easy, and is best served with fluffy white rice, some natural yoghurt and a crunchy salad.

Feeds 4

1. Place the meat and onion in a saucepan and pour in the cold water. Add the turmeric and pepper and stir well. Place a lid on the pan and simmer for 20 minutes over a low heat.

2. Meanwhile, skin the tomatoes by scoring the skins with a sharp knife a few times and placing them in a bowl of just-boiled water for about a minute. Drain well, then rub off the skin. Cut the tomatoes in half, remove and discard the seeds, then cut into small dice.

3. Add the diced tomato to the pan, along with the tomato purée, cayenne and salt, followed by the oil. Simmer with the lid on for another 15 minutes, stirring occasionally, and then cook for 5 minutes with the lid off until the sauce has the consistency of a thick ragu.

4. Crack the eggs into the pan and leave to set for a minute. Gently run a wooden spoon through the yolks a few times. Don't mix too much, as you want to have chunks of egg in the final dish, not scrambled eggs. Place a lid on until the eggs are set and then taste to adjust the seasoning.

5. Serve with the spring onions sprinkled on top.

IRMA

Born: *Brownsville, Texas, USA, 1941*
Mother tongue: *Spanish*
Grandchildren: *Nicolás, Logan*
They call her: *Grandma*

MEAT

We went to track down Irma at her eponymous Tex-Mex restaurant, Irma's Original. The sign outside read 'Comida como en su casa' - food just like at home. The restaurant was in a parking lot in central Houston with corrugated walls, Bud Light signs and Mexican wind chimes. Inside was packed with people dipping tortillas, downing margaritas and forking beautiful combinations into taco shells.

The tables were covered in a mad assortment of plastic covers, from snakeskin to bright floral to leopard print. Baseball memorabilia, photos of Irma winning prizes, neon signs and trinkets lined the walls and one room was entirely festooned with Christmas lights - a flashing web across the whole ceiling. This is Irma's bold, fun style, which was confirmed the following day at her own home.

Irma was firm, sure and matter-of-fact, which perhaps comes from raising kids and running a successful business on her own. There was a team of great women behind her, two of whom were there to help prep the immense Tex-Mex feast. We could have sat and clinked lime-plugged Coronas with Irma and her pals all night.

When we were little my mother would cook this for us. I made it with her when I was just a kid. I never met my father and we were raised by my mother alone, so we didn't have much money growing up. I'm the oldest of four and I was the one tasked with helping my mother. She'd give me a dollar to go to the store and buy the meat for picadillos, then we'd stand and make this together. We'd eat this with rice, and the next day we might have it in some tacos or in a tortilla with avocado. You have to make do with what you have. That's the Mexican way.

Now I love to host and to have parties. At Cinco de Mayo I had 200 people at my home. I like to entertain, which is probably why

I have my own restaurant. I opened Irma's in 1989 and we're still going. We get people coming from all over the world. I even won a James Beard Award. It was such an honour but I still accepted my award dressed in my shorts and apron.

In Texas we tweak the traditional Mexican dishes because of the abundance of cattle. There's so much beef that there's no escaping it in our cuisine. We still consider this to be Mexican because in spite of growing up in Texas, we were raised Mexican and that means making one small meal go a long way.

I don't go back to where my mother was born because these places are deep in Mexico and they're dangerous. I was born very close to the border with Mexico in South Texas and that place itself is now a risky place to live. It's where a lot of drugs cross between.

There's a little friction between the Mexicans that live in Mexico and those that live in Texas. They feel we have it made here in the US. Maybe we do, but we have worked hard to make it that way. People in Mexico are humble, hardworking and they come up here for the 'American Dream' that everybody talks about.

When I was a little girl I didn't have anything. I admired people that had nice things. I hoped I would one day be like them. Now I have my own business and five houses of my own. I am a person that wants to get ahead. I'm a leader and I'm only going to retire when God decides to retire me.

I was 21 years old when I married and 29 when he died. They murdered him at a bar. He was celebrating New Year's Eve and was shot while I was at home with our kids making *tamales*. He was supposed to be at home. It's a Mexican custom - being with the family, making *tamales* and gathering to eat at midnight. They didn't find him until the next day. We were waiting for him, but two detectives came knocking at nine o'clock in the morning. My youngest child was just five years old. We were devastated.

What I believe is that men come and go but your friends will always be there. Without my girls, I'm nothing. We work together as a team. We taste each other's cooking. We've been cooking together for decades. I depend on them, they depend on me. At work, we're all like family. No one is an employee. They're just all my girls. It's not about me being the big boss. I work alongside everyone and we do this thing together. It's so important to love your people if you're delegating and managing or head of a company. You have to be strong but forgiving and you have to be together with them. I eat with my girls every day. There's not one day I would eat without them. 1.30 p.m., it's lunch for us all. Together.
—

Grandma Irma

GRANDMA IRMA'S
TEX-MEX BEEF TACOS

INGREDIENTS
(Feeds 4-6)

— 1 tbsp rapeseed oil
— 400g (14oz) minced beef
— 1 tsp ground cumin
— 2 garlic cloves, finely chopped
— 1 green chilli, chopped (Irma uses a
  similar native chilli called serrano)
— 1 small carrot, diced into 0.5cm (¼in)
  cubes
— 1 floury potato, diced into 1cm (½in)
  cubes
— 1 small onion, peeled and quartered
— 1 green pepper, roughly chopped
— 1 red pepper, roughly chopped
— 1 fresh tomato, diced (optional)
— 2 spring onions, chopped
— 1 x 400g (14oz) tin chopped
  tomatoes
— 1 tbsp tomato purée
— 1 handful fresh coriander, chopped,
  plus extra to serve
— 8 traditional Mexican corn tortillas,
  4 soft corn tortillas (to make your
  own) or 8 pre-made hard taco shells
— vegetable oil, for deep frying,
  if needed

METHOD

1. In a large pan heat the rapeseed oil over a medium flame and put the minced beef into the sizzling oil. Break up the meat with a wooden spoon while it browns for a few minutes.

2. Once browned a little all over, season generously with sea salt and freshly ground black pepper. Reduce the heat slightly and stir in the cumin, garlic and green chilli.

3. Next add the veg: the carrot, potato, quartered onion, peppers, fresh tomato and spring onions. Stir to combine.

4. Empty the tin of tomatoes into the pan followed by half a tin of water and the tomato purée. Stir again, taste and season more if it needs it, cover with a lid and cook for 20 minutes.

5. When the time is up, throw in the handful of coriander and leave to cook for a further 5 minutes.

6. To make the tacos, Irma put soft 15cm (6in) corn tortillas into a pan of hot oil, pushed down the middle of the tortilla with a fork and cooked until golden to make it into a folded taco shape for piling filling in. Try this yourself with the larger soft tortillas you can buy in the UK or use shop-bought hard taco shells and add your beef filling. Irma served hers with guacamole, rice, beans and salsa.

SOMETHING

SWEET

DOLORES

Dolores only told us what we'd be cooking with her on the day of our arrival in Lafayette, a swamp-surrounded town, deep in Louisiana. When we heard the words 'pig's ears', we looked at each other in alarm. We usually check in with the grandmothers in advance to talk over their recipe, but Dolores was one of the most impromptu grandmas we've cooked with, so we didn't quite have the time to on this occasion.

Anastasia cracked out the 'I don't eat pork' line she falls back on whenever a slightly unsavoury piggy snack is proffered by a grandma, and Dolores chuckled.

It transpired that the 80-year-old makes her pig's ears from a cannoli-type crispy pastry, then drizzles them in sticky cane syrup and crushed pecans. Cane syrup is prolific in the area and has been popular since the plantation days, when Dolores' ancestors arrived in the boggy wetlands of Louisiana.

We crunched down on them at what can only be described as a lively barn dance at Vermilionville, a historic reenactment village, made only stranger by the odd 16th-century French being spoken in 'Cajun Country' by just about everyone we met there.

Born: *Broussard, Louisiana, USA, 1947*
Mother tongue: *American English*
Grandchild: *Millicent*
She calls her: *Miss D*

This dessert is a lot of fun. When I said I was cooking these for an event, I was told to change the recipe 'because a lot of people really don't like pork'. Oh, I thought it was so funny. I had a good laugh. Of course it isn't actually a real pig's ear.

I love cooking. I first started when I was probably 16 years old. My mother and my older siblings did a lot of cooking. I was the baby of the family so I really didn't do too, too much at all. It was, 'Sit down and watch and don't ask too, too many questions.'

I just started cooking because I was interested. These pig's ears are typical of the area, but it's a very rare recipe that got lost. There was only one other lady in the neighbourhood that used to make these. I like the idea that I'm reviving it.

I was a cafeteria cook at a high school for 32 years and oh my, do I love to cook. I retired 15 years ago but I still cook for community events and the like. You have to keep yourself occupied. Also, if you want to retire, you really have to save money – even if you don't want to do any travelling. You have really got to think and plan for your future.

I personally love to travel. It's so important to see how other people live. It's one of the best ways to grow in life. I went to Nicaragua and I thought, Some of the youths of America need to go to there and see how they live. They would count their blessings more. They'd be on their knees.

Obviously my great-grandparents were slaves and following that their descendants were working in the fields and were housekeepers, but I really believe that you can feel the racial tensions in these parts much more now than we did back when I was younger. Things have changed a lot in the course of a lifetime here in Louisiana.

The Civil Rights Movement happened when we were young children. I was at a black school to begin with. Then it was closed and we were transferred to a mixed one right across the street. That was when I was integrated, as they say. I was just a young girl – only nine years old. I didn't really feel a threat at all at the time. Not from white kids or their parents. It was really OK. I got along with all children in the playground. Children really don't see colour. Adults see it all much worse.

Everybody knew everybody else in the town, so my parents weren't worried about my attending an integrated school. We were all more accepting. When I was growing up it wasn't bad. It wasn't like it is now. There is a definite racial divide here now. Black guys chase white women. They treat them different. They treat them better than black women. That's just one small example of what causes tensions between the races.

You can really feel the tension and a hostility now. It would be wonderful if we could not see colour and only see people. A bit like what things were like back when I was at school, in the playground.
—

Miss D

MISS D'S PASTRY PIG'S EARS

INGREDIENTS
(Makes 16)

— 350g (2½ cups) plain flour,
  plus extra for rolling
— 1 tsp baking powder
— ½ tsp salt
— 2 large eggs
— 8 tbsp butter, melted
  and cooled slightly
— splash milk
— vegetable oil (for deep
  frying)
— 150ml (⅔ cup) sugar syrup
  (300g/1½ cups caster
  sugar dissolved into 150ml/
  ⅔ cup water over low heat)
— 175ml (½ cup) blackstrap
  molasses (black treacle,
  date syrup or honey also
  work)
— 100g (1 cup) pecans, toasted
  and chopped (you can also
  use walnuts or hazelnuts)

METHOD

1. Sift together the flour, baking powder and salt and set aside.

2. In another bowl beat the eggs with a whisk until frothy. Add the cooled melted butter while beating, then change to a spoon and fold into the flour mixture in four parts – a dough will form. Use your hands to bring the dough together and add a tiny splash of milk if the mixture is too dry – it should be firm and smooth, not crumbling or particularly sticky.

3. Divide the dough into 16 equal portions and roll each one into a ball about 2.5cm (1in) in diameter.

4. On a lightly floured surface, use a rolling pin to roll each ball out into a paper-thin circle, about 20cm (8in) in diameter. Just when you think it's thin enough, stop and roll again – it's really important to get the pastry as thin as possible. It should be translucent. Trim the edges with a knife to reinstate the circle if you like to keep things neat.

5. Pour 3cm (1¼in) of vegetable oil into a sauté pan. Heat to 170°C (340°F), if you have a thermometer, or until bubbles quickly form around your wooden spoon when you dip the end in the oil.

6. Carefully peel your pastry off the surface and slide into the pan. Working quickly, immediately stick a fork into the middle and twist (not too hard, you don't want to break the pastry). Keep twirling as the pastry folds around itself to resemble a pig's ear – as you twirl you may want to position your fork so the pastry is brushing the edge of the pan, as this can help make the shape.

7. When the 'pig's ear' has formed and set a little, keep the fork in place until the pastry begins to brown lightly. It should take around 30 seconds to turn golden brown. When you are happy with the colour, flip and brown the other side. Remove with tongs or a slotted spoon, letting the excess oil drip. Move to a lined baking tray to cool and harden; repeat with remaining circles and don't be disheartened if you mess up the first one – it gets easier!

8. When you've fried all the circles and they've fully cooled, mix the syrup and molasses together and drizzle over, followed by a sprinkling of nuts.

Grandmother Florence Tyan's Irish Butter Sponge Cake

Darina Allen, founder of Ballymaloe Cookery School

Ingredients

— 125g (½ cup + 1 tbsp) butter
— 175g (¾ cup) caster sugar
— 3 eggs, organic and
  free-range (important!)
— 175g (1¼ cups) flour
— 1 tsp baking powder
— 1 tbsp milk

Filling

— 110g (½ cup) homemade
  raspberry jam
— 300ml (1¼ cups) double
  cream, whipped
— caster sugar to sprinkle

My maternal grandmother, Florence Tyan, was by all accounts a renowned cook. I inherited her recipe for a buttery sponge cake. This was a favourite to serve for afternoon tea at my grandmother's house in Donoughmore, near Johnstown in County Kilkenny.

When it was taken out of the Aga, it was cooled on a wire rack by the open window in the back kitchen. Thick yellow cream, spooned off the top of the milk in the dairy, was lightly whipped. As soon as the cake was cool it was sandwiched together with the cream and homemade jam made from the raspberries picked at the top of the haggard. Believe me, this is the best sponge cake you'll ever taste. It is best served on an old-fashioned plate with a doily.

This cake will be even better if you make your own jam. Raspberry jam is the easiest and quickest of all jams to make, and one of the most delicious.

Feeds 8-10

1. Preheat oven to 190°C/170°C fan/375°F/gas 5.

2. Grease 2 x 18cm (7in) sponge-cake tins with melted butter, dust with flour and line the base of each with a round of greaseproof paper.

3. Cream the butter and gradually add the caster sugar, beating until soft and light and quite pale in colour.

4. Add the eggs one at a time and beat well between each addition. (If the butter and sugar are not creamed properly and if you add the eggs too fast, the mixture will curdle, resulting in a cake with a heavier texture.)

5. Sieve the flour and baking powder and stir in gradually. Mix all together lightly and add 1 tbsp of milk to moisten.

6. Divide the mixture evenly between the 2 tins, hollowing it slightly in the centre. Bake in the preheated oven for 20–25 minutes or until cooked – the cake will shrink in slightly from the edge of the tin when it is cooked; the centre should feel exactly the same texture as the edge. Alternatively, a skewer should come out clean when put into the centre of the cake.

7. Turn out onto a wire tray and allow to cool.

8. Sandwich the two bases together with homemade raspberry jam and whipped cream. Sprinkle with sieved caster sugar.

WESTELLE

The day before we met Westelle, we were in Nashville with two broken cameras and managed to track down a Canon specialist. The Canon specialist was Gary, and while he didn't manage to fix the cameras, he fixed us up with his mother Westelle, muffin maker extraordinaire. The following day Gary collected us in his red Jeep and we drove out into the hills between the November trees in an incredible palette of yellow, orange and red, in and out of small towns, past enormous churches and most notably a sign praising 'God, family & chicken nuggets'.

Westelle was waiting at the door, a tiny figure behind a billowing American flag, make-up done and hair set. Family photographs and cross-stitched quotes covered every inch of the bungalow she designed with her late husband. A copy of *To Kill a Mockingbird* was poised beside the toilet on a spotless marble dresser, her fridge was so large she could have hung out inside it, and her hand whisk was from 1981.

We sat on her counter as she whisked flour, buttermilk, sugar and an entire box of Raisin Bran, saying, 'Well, ain't you girls precious?' and talking of princes William and Harry as if they were family. Her hands were so arthritic but she didn't complain. 'I've really had a good life,' she said, and we welled up at her admittance, that, at 92, it's almost all up. Still, she was determined that we come back for Thanksgiving because she was hosting and cooking for 20. Power to Westelle.

Born: *Shelbyville, Tennessee, USA, 1927*
Mother tongue: *American English*
Grandchildren: *Chris, Jason, Steffie, Maggie, Scott, Jonathan, Luke, Garrett, Ian, Wesley*
They call her: *Grandmother*

I think I learned this recipe from a neighbour, but it must have been way back in the 1950s that I first baked these muffins. I have things in my kitchen that are over 50 years old – my cake mixer, for example. I believe in holding on to things when they work good. Why get rid of it if it still works?

I have always cooked and I don't see any sense in stopping just because I'm old. Yesterday morning I had bacon and toast and some scrambled egg. I eat really well. Some of my friends who are younger than me will go out to eat for every meal. It's nice to do that, but I think it's important to cook your own meals, even at my age.

I never use the word 'old'. I was taking this Bible class and it was mostly ladies, and this woman whose face looked like a prune was sitting beside me. Her hair was dyed bright red like a fire truck. I was wearing a jacket and the ladies in the class complimented me on it. Anyway, this lady looked over at me and said, 'you're old and in denial.' Needless to say, I didn't go back to that class any more. I could not believe it. Can you believe it? In a Bible class – to have that treatment. I didn't think it was at all funny.

I go to the gym two days a week. I go to the Christian widowed women's group. I also take turmeric capsules, which I absolutely swear by. I still drive. I have a Chevrolet Impala. It's a super-size car but I have cushions I sit on. When it's cleaned up, it looks pretty good.

I don't think about age. I just keep myself busy. I always have done.

I really took on a lot of responsibility with the three boys at home and my husband busy at work. They ate so much. They'd get through a gallon of milk perhaps in one day. When they were in school, they all liked different breakfasts. Gary would want sausages and scrambled eggs, Randy would like toast and wheat spread, and Steve only wanted pancakes. So I would get up and cook all of these different breakfasts for the kids every day before they went to school. They never went to school without breakfast.

I hate to say this but it's true: there are a lot of mothers in contemporary America that are too lazy to get up and feed their children. I really do think it's a sin. They have to see to it that their children have a balanced diet. If you can't do that most basic thing, you're not much of a mom, in my opinion.

Almost all my siblings are deceased but my youngest sister is alive. She has dementia and is really not well. She is in a hospice now because she's that bad. She really was the sweetest, kindest thing. I am 12 years older than her and I would treat her like my own baby. It's just such a shame.

I have rheumatoid arthritis but I never say anything because I look around and see all these people who are diabetic and who have heart problems. You're just blessed if you can get up every day. I don't dwell on things too much. I'm at an age now where I've had a lot of loss. You can't do anything about it and the things you can't do anything about, you have to find peace with. I think about the people I've lost all the time, but I focus on all the beautiful things we've lived together. I've really had a good life. You just make the best of whatever.

—

Grandmother Westelle

GRANDMOTHER WESTELLE'S SOUTHERN PECAN AND CRANBERRY BUTTERMILK MUFFINS

INGREDIENTS
(Makes 12)

— 2 eggs
— 120ml (½ cup) vegetable oil
— 250ml (1 cup + 1 tbsp) buttermilk
— 250g (1¼ cups) caster sugar, plus extra to sprinkle
— 1 tsp salt
— 400g (2¾ cups) self-raising flour
— 50g (½ cup) pecans, roughly chopped
— 50g (⅓ cup) dried cranberries
— 2 handfuls bran flakes with raisins

METHOD

1. Line a 12-hole muffin tin with 12 large muffin cases and preheat oven to 190°C/170°C fan/375°F/gas 5.

2. In a large mixing bowl use an electric whisk to beat the eggs until fluffy.

3. Add the vegetable oil and buttermilk and whisk until well blended.

4. Add the caster sugar and whisk again. Follow with the salt and flour – whisk once more, stopping as soon as the flour is combined.

5. Next add the pecans, cranberries and raisin bran (crumble the pieces of bran slightly with your hand as you go). Fold in gently.

6. Divide the batter between the cases and sprinkle the tops with the extra sugar. Bake for about 20-25 minutes until golden and risen. A skewer inserted into the centre of a muffin should come out clean.

7. Remove the muffins from the oven and transfer to a wire rack to cool for at least 30 minutes before eating.

Tip: If you can't get buttermilk, you can use natural yoghurt or stir 1 tbsp lemon juice into 240ml (1 cup) whole milk and leave for 5 minutes to sour before using in the recipe.

Nonna Elsa's Italian Fior di Latte Gelato

Sophia Brothers, founder of Nonna's Gelato

Ingredients

— 650ml (2¾ cups) whole milk
— 120ml (½ cup) double cream
— 180g (heaped ¾ cup) unrefined sugar
— 45g (3 tbsp) skimmed milk powder
— 1 tsp cornflour

My Nonna has always made everything from scratch, from rolling pasta out on the kitchen table to infusing lemon rind in alcohol for months on end to make the best limoncello I've ever tasted. She inspired me to start my own food business in London and make fine Italian gelato.

While she sadly doesn't cook any more, I will forever remember her pottering around in the kitchen and watching her prepare endless feasts for all her family and four granddaughters. The smells and aromas that filled her Mediterranean kitchen will always be present. I am sharing her recipe for *fior di latte* gelato, a very traditional Italian milk flavour that literally translates as 'flower of milk'. It is where I started when adapting and creating my own recipes. You'll need a probe thermometer and plenty of ice to make an ice bath.

Feeds about 11

1. Place the milk and cream in a saucepan over medium heat. While it's warming, place the sugar, skimmed milk powder and cornflour in a measuring jug and mix well.

2. Using a probe thermometer, measure the temperature of the milk and cream. When it reaches 40°C (104°F), add the dry ingredients. Whisk together and stir continuously with a heatproof spatula until it reaches 85°C (185°F).

3. Fill the sink with ice and cold water to create an ice bath. Plunge the saucepan into the ice bath and stir occasionally. You need to bring the temperature down to 10°C (50°F) within 30 minutes.

4. When the mix is cooled, place in a sealed container and refrigerate for at least 4 hours, but preferably overnight.

5. You're now ready to churn it into gelato. Start by passing it through a fine sieve.

6. Blitz with a hand blender.

7. Pour into your ice-cream machine and churn until frozen.

8. Scoop your freshly churned gelato into a container and cover with greaseproof paper and a tight-fitting lid. Place in the freezer and consume within 1 month.

ANIA

Babcia Ania made us *pampuchy*, a Polish steamed dumpling similar to bao buns. They can be eaten sweet or savoury. It's the dish her grandchildren always ask for when they go to visit her.

She usually lives in an apartment in Suwałki, but the family decided that our cooking adventure should happen at her daughter's home just outside Poznań due to size. The house was surrounded by forests and was a half-hour drive from the lake where we all went for a late-afternoon swim.

On *pampuchy* day Babcia had 14 mouths to feed. This meant we ate in two 'loads' at the table while Babcia established a very successful production line steaming a round of buns while others rose. We ate them first with a rich pork and onion stew called *gulasz*, using the fluffy buns to soak up the gravy. Then we ate them with the blueberry sauce - made with blueberries we'd watched her barter for with serious gusto at the market in Poznań that morning.

Born: *Suwałki, Poland, 1931*
Mother tongue: *Polish*
Grandchildren: *Marcin, Magdalena, Karina, Krzysztof, Urszula, Jakub, Michał, Carla, Arthur*
They call her: *Babcia*

I've loved being in nature ever since I was a child. We'd venture into the forests of Poland's Masuria region, famous for its thousands of lakes, and fill two huge pails with wild blueberries from the forest, seal some of them in glass jars and then boil the jars in hot water to make a stash for the winter. The rest we would enjoy in situ while foraging or for lunch that same afternoon with *pampuchy* (steamed buns), *naleśniki* (blintzes) or even *zupa jagodowa* (blueberry soup).

These early memories were amongst the happiest I passed in that place. When the Second World War arrived, trips to the forest took on a different tone under Nazi fascism. At the beginning, we saw the Germans as good people. I remember in 1941, they stationed soldiers in our house and one of them brought me an orange because he said that I reminded him of his daughter. It got much worse later on, unfortunately.

My father was part of Armia Krajowa (the Polish Home Army), a subversive group of Poles that fought against the Germans during the entirety of the war. My mother was a liaison. Liaisons were undercover women, men and children, without whom there would not have been a Home Army. The AK, made up of men, hid out in the forests sometimes for weeks at a time. They put makeshift explosives on trains, built large weapons and worked with the British against the occupying Germans. I eventually learned that I conspired with the AK myself, but at the time I had no idea.

My mother would put notes in my bag and tell me to go into the forest and wait under the largest oak tree in a certain field. As I walked into the forest, German officers would ask me what I was doing. My mother told me to tell them, 'I'm going to the forest to gather nuts.' I'd then wait under the oak tree and an AK would come running from the deeper forest to get the notes from me. I wasn't scared because I didn't even know what I was doing. I just knew to do as I was told. Many children were used as liaisons, passing reports, tools, and parcels, because the Germans were less likely to kill them.

One night a German came into our house looking for my father. They pushed my mother around with their gun, pinned her against the wall and demanded to know where her husband was. We three kids just started bawling and screeching, to the point where the Germans couldn't handle it any more. They threatened to shoot my mother but in the end, they let her go, probably because our crying really shook them.

Life wasn't perfect after the war, but it had to go on - there were children to feed and work to do. We were then under a Russian shadow until 1989 - they drove everything. Before our access to the free market, it was practically impossible to travel out of the country. Food was closely monitored and ration cards were allocated. There were long queues to collect groceries, so it was much better to grow our own. We all were curious as to what life was like on the outside. There was a radio station called Radio Wolna Europa (Radio Free Europe) and we listened to it illegally to learn about the democratic world.

I left for the first time in 1974 and went to America. My cousin Rysia secured a visa for me. I had to receive approval from the government first, so my cousin had to write a letter stating that she worked at a travel agency and that she would cover all the costs. All I was allowed to take with me from Poland was a single $20 note.

When I arrived, the first thing I did was ask my cousin to take me to a grocery store just to look at the full shelves. I had never seen anything like it. We were so closely monitored though, I wasn't allowed to bring anything back. On my return, I was interrogated. 'Are the Americans slandering the Poles? What did you do in America? Who were you with? How did you travel around? What did you eat?' are the types of questions they asked me.

When communism ended here in 1989, we were all ecstatic to finally have democracy. Now Poland is the complete opposite of what it was. It's beautiful. Food is abundant. We take part in international trade, importing and exporting. We can travel the whole world without limitation.
—

Babcia Ania

BABCIA ANIA'S POLISH STEAMED BUNS WITH BLUEBERRY SAUCE (*Pampuchy*)

INGREDIENTS
(*Makes 10-12 large buns*)

- 500ml (2¼ cups) milk
- 30g (1oz) fresh yeast (you can also use 3 tsp dried yeast, but Ania prefers fresh)
- 2 tsp granulated sugar
- 500g (3½ cups) plain flour, plus 3 tbsp extra for the milk pan
- ½ tsp sea salt
- 2 medium eggs, beaten
- 1 tbsp vegetable oil

FOR THE SAUCE

- 400g (3 cups) blueberries (fresh, or frozen and defrosted)
- 2 tbsp granulated sugar

METHOD

1. Warm the milk gently in a medium saucepan. Take off the heat and transfer ⅔ of the milk into a jug and set aside (you will need this to loosen the dough with later).

2. Crumble the fresh yeast into the pan and stir in the sugar and 3 tbsp flour. The mixture should be the consistency of double cream. Put a lid on the pan and leave on the kitchen counter to double in size.

3. Meanwhile, combine the 500g (3½ cups) flour and the salt in a big mixing bowl and pour the eggs into a well in the centre.

4. Once the mixture in the saucepan has doubled (about 6 minutes), pour it into the well too. You can tip a little of the extra milk into the pan to swish out the remaining yeast if you like.

5. Mix everything together with a spoon to combine; this is where you may need to add more of the warm milk, a little bit at a time – you want it to be a firm but sticky dough that easily forms a ball. Then start to knead – you can use a little bit of flour to coat the dough so it's easier to handle, but try not to add too much more, as it could make your buns less fluffy. Ania says to knead and beat the dough with your whole arm strength for about 5 minutes until smooth and stiff with no lumps.

6. Add the oil and take another minute or so to incorporate it. Now the dough should be soft and shiny. Sprinkle with flour and cover with a clean, damp tea towel. Leave in a warm spot to rise for 20 minutes. Ania says that in the summer this might be quicker, and the opposite for the winter.

7. Keep a few blueberries aside for decoration and whizz the rest together with the sugar in a bowl using a hand blender. Some people cook the blueberries down, but Ania likes to blend them from fresh.

8. Once it's risen, turn the dough out onto a floured surface. Shape into a long, even sausage shape. Cut this length into 10–12 equal pieces (they should be about palm-sized) and roll into balls between your hands, tucking floury sides inside if they are stopping the ball from taking shape. Space the balls out as you go, and when you're done, cover with a tea towel and leave for 5 minutes to rise. Either use a steamer pan or build your own, like Babcia, who filled her saucepan with 2cm (¾in) of hot water and covered it with a clean cotton tea towel held taut with string – this will be the steaming platform. Put on a medium heat.

9. Pop the buns in batches onto the steaming platform 3cm (1¼in) apart, cover with a lid (or if you've gone DIY, with an upturned similar-sized saucepan or metal bowl) and steam for 10 minutes. If you're using a metal steamer you may want to lightly rub with oil to stop the buns sticking.

10. When done, remove the buns from the steamer onto plates, leave to rest for a minute, serve with a drizzle of the blueberry sauce and a few fresh blueberries on top.

Tip: If you've made more than you can eat, these keep really well in the freezer. To revive them, simply defrost at room temperature and return to the steamer pan for a few minutes before serving.

SOMETHING SWEET

Mormor Elsa's Swedish Chocolate Cake (*Kladdkaka*)

Emma Bengtsson, chef

Ingredients

— 175g (6oz) dark chocolate
— 175g (¾ cup) butter
— 4 eggs
— 320g (heaped 1½ cups) caster sugar
— 120g (heaped ¾ cup) plain flour
— 40g (7½ tbsp) cocoa powder

My grandmother lived in a small town called Svedala in the south of Sweden. We used to go there to visit on holidays and in the summer. My favourite part was when I first stepped into her place and the amazing aromas of food would hit me. From the steak, potatoes, and carrots dripping with butter to the sweet smell from the chocolate cake in the oven. I still have her original handwritten recipe at home. I don't remember specifically when she gave it to me, but I tear up every time I see it. She would always bake it for me when I came over to visit and I know she wrote the recipe down for me so that I could start baking it myself.

I have baked this cake – *Kladdkaka* – thousands of times and it is still one of my favourite things to make. I wish that I could get the chance to meet her again so that I could tell her how much she inspired me to become who I am today. She was the one that planted the seed in me to become a chef. In the early parts of my career, she was still here with us and she was so proud of me.

She was a strong and stubborn woman who was also very kind and thoughtful. My mum is just the same and I hope that people see me that way as well. There is not a day that goes by where I don't think about her. And the recipe of her favourite chocolate cake will always be on my menu. A reminder to be strong but also kind.

Makes 1 cake

1. Preheat oven to 160°C/140°C fan/325°F/gas 3.

2. Break the chocolate into small pieces and put into a heatproof bowl.

3. Melt the butter in a pan and pour it over the chocolate. Make sure that all the chocolate is melted before moving on.

4. Whisk the eggs and sugar together. It should not become fluffy.

5. Fold the chocolate and butter into the egg and sugar mixture.

6. Sift the flour and cocoa powder together and then fold into the egg and chocolate mix.

7. Grease a 20–25cm (8–10in) cake mould, pour the cake mix into the mould and place it into the oven for about 35–45 minutes. Every oven is different and therefore it is hard to set a precise time. It should still be a bit undercooked in the middle.

8. Remove from the oven and let cool down before removing from the mould.

9. Serve with whipped cream and fresh berries or jam if it's wintertime.

NICOLE

We were introduced to Nicole through her son Alfred (master mixologist and heir to the Cointreau empire). The family kindly sent us Eurostar train tickets and hosted us at their beautiful home in Angers. On arrival we made our way down a long, tree-lined driveway to an old converted barn with a bright, open kitchen at its core.

The whole weekend was a poem in orange: giant pumpkins in the greenhouse, Nicole's Cointreau-colour-matched skirt, the iconic orange of the Cointreau bottle, and an army of us in the kitchen juicing oranges for *tarte d'oranges*. It was November but we spent our time outdoors, wading through a thick leaf carpet to find the right shot of Nicole amongst the autumn trees, baby granddaughter Louison to incite extra giggles.

Nicole and her husband spoke limited English but we seamlessly laid the table in unison and all sat down together, using food as a medium for hilarity and storytelling. Cultural differences were showcased when the cheeseboard came to us first and we cut hunks of fromage double the size of theirs; 'hungry English girls' isn't a very classy title.

This is, however, a classy little tart. It can be made with or without Cointreau and served with afternoon tea or as a dessert.

Born: *Angers, France, 1958*
Mother tongue: *French*
Grandchildren: *Eleanore, Emma, Louison*
They call her: *Grand Maman*

My grandmother used to make this orange tart. It's her recipe and I learned to cook it in her kitchen with my 12 aunts. It was always such a busy kitchen. I was essentially raised by my grandmothers. They'd always say, 'Keep your husband by cooking him good food.' When I married François (Cointreau) I started adding Cointreau to the recipe as a sort of new twist on the classic. Most families in this region of France have a bottle of Cointreau in the house though, so it was hardly a drastic change to the traditional tart.

I first met my husband at a party. We were only 17 and it was a soirée for society children, arranged by our parents so we could meet other children from 'good' families, as they would put it. On one occasion

there happened to be a power cut and a friend began playing piano in the dark. I was sitting next to François and he turned his head as I turned mine. That was our first kiss. I had a feeling then that he was the man I would marry.

I remember we both had a Solex – a kind of bike with an engine – and we'd ride out next to each other on them and try to kiss. On one occasion, our front wheels touched and of course we ended up crashing. The brake wire snapped on my scooter and whipped me across the face. My parents were so scared I'd be scarred for life they sent me to the village soothsayer, who put calla lillies marinated in alcohol on my face every day for months. I don't have a single mark on my face now.

Three weeks after we met, my father tried to scare François off by saying I wouldn't be given a dowry. My parents were so worried I was too young for a boyfriend that they sent me to boarding school in England. Of course, François waited for me.

When we married we went to see a priest and the priest told us to always agree in front of our children. We have always followed that advice. After 34 years we understand each other. We know what the other's thinking. I think the key has been to listen and to always talk. Every day you can turn to the other person and tell them it's over; the hardest thing to do is to decide that it's going to work and that you'll make it work.
—

Grand Maman Nicole

GRAND MAMAN NICOLE'S FRENCH ORANGE TART WITH COINTREAU (*Tarte d'oranges*)

INGREDIENTS
(Feeds 8-10)

— 150g (⅔ cup) unsalted butter, softened
— 100g (½ cup) caster sugar
— 1 egg
— 200g (heaped 1⅓ cups) flour

FOR THE FILLING

— 100g (½ cup) caster sugar
— 2 large eggs
— juice of 2 oranges
— 2 tbsp Cointreau

FOR THE TOPPING

— 2 oranges
— brown sugar for dusting

METHOD

1. Preheat oven to 180°C/160°C fan/350°F/gas 4 and grease a 25cm (10in) tart tin or dish and set aside.

2. Cream the softened butter and sugar together in a bowl, then beat in the egg until well combined.

3. Slowly mix in the flour and a pinch of salt until the mixture comes together. Shape the dough into a disc (this will make it easier to spread out into your tart case later), wrap in cling film and chill for 30 minutes in the fridge to firm up a little.

4. Meanwhile make the tart filling. Whizz the sugar and eggs together in a blender, add the orange juice and Cointreau and blend again – it will be quite a liquidy mix, but that's OK. Set aside.

5. Next slice the top and bottom off the oranges you're using for the topping with a sharp knife, so you have a flat base to sit them on. Then slice down the sides to remove all the peel and cut the orange into 3mm (⅛in)-thick rounds (each orange should make about 8).

6. Once chilled, unwrap your dough and place it into the base of your tart tin. Use your fingertips to gently push the dough, coaxing it up the sides so it covers the tin evenly. Cut off any excess dough and prick all over with a fork.

7. Fill the tart case with crumpled greaseproof paper and baking beans (or dried pulses). Place in the oven and bake for 15 minutes. Remove the paper and beans and cook for a further 5 minutes or until slightly browned. Don't be alarmed if the sides shrink a little.

8. Next, pour the filling into the tart case and arrange the orange slices on top (they will sink – not a problem). Return to the oven for a further 20 minutes and when the filling is almost set, sprinkle a generous layer of brown sugar over the top of the dish. Return to the oven for another 10 minutes, until set and the sugar has caramelised on top.

9. Leave for a few minutes to cool a little, then serve warm or cold with chocolate mousse, ice cream or cream.

Tip: Nicole has a special spray bottle of Cointreau, and she finishes this tart off with a single spray. Copy her and make one at home for a final burst of bright, bitter, zesty orange.

Gampie Paula's Australian Apple Pie

Maxine Thompson, founder of PolkaPants chefs' clothing

For the pastry

— 400g (2¾ cups) plain flour, plus extra for rolling
— 2 tbsp caster sugar
— zest of 1 lemon
— 250g (1 cup + 2 tbsp) butter, cold and cut into cubes
— 2 eggs, beaten separately
— 2 tbsp cold water

For the filling

— 150g (¾ cup) golden caster sugar, plus extra for sprinkling
— 1 tsp ground cinnamon
— 600g (1lb 5oz) cooking apples, peeled, cored, roughly chopped into pieces

When I think of my grandmother (Gampie) I think of matching twin-set suits, silk headscarves, blouses and brandy. Paula Thompson was a walking piece of art. She was cool and hilarious at the same time. She was petite and cheeky. Men fell in love with her and the younger generations adored her. She was the hostess with the mostest and was often the last man standing at a party. She was fashionable at all times and was a true bohemian who truly cherished her grandchildren.

She loved food, travelled a lot and cooked whenever she had the chance. Her ability to knock up an apple pie in the blink of an eye made her the envy of her friends. Gampie loved to cook this because the prep time versus the delight it brings is minimal. She loved it because you could chop apples haphazardly and throw the pastry together. She would much prefer to entertain than be in the kitchen.

My fondest memories with her were spending balmy summer afternoons in her tiny apartment in Rose Bay (Sydney), watching the tennis, drinking lemonade and eating ladyfinger biscuits, musk sweets and melted chocolate ice cream.

Feeds 8-10

1. For the pastry, place the flour, sugar, lemon zest and pinch of salt into a bowl. Rub in the butter until the mixture resembles breadcrumbs. Add one beaten egg and 2 tbsp cold water and stir with a round-blade knife until the mixture forms a dough. Set aside ⅓ of the pastry for the lid.

2. For the pie base you can use the traditional method of rolling out the pastry dough, or you can grate the dough directly into the pie dish and press it firmly into the sides (this is a less fussy way of creating the base and less frustrating!). If using the rolling method, roll out the remaining pastry on a floured surface until the thickness of a pound coin and 6cm (2½in) larger than the pie dish. Lift the pastry over the rolling pin and lower it gently into the pie dish.

3. Press the pastry firmly into the dish and up the sides, making sure there are no air bubbles. Chill in the fridge for 15 minutes.

4. Preheat oven to 200°C/180°C fan/400°F/gas 6 and place a baking tray into the oven.

5. For the filling, mix the sugar and cinnamon in a large bowl. Stir in the apples. Place the apple filling into the pie dish, making sure that it rises above the edge. Brush the rim with beaten egg.

6. Roll out the reserved ball of pastry. Cover the pie with the pastry and press the edges together firmly to seal. Using a sharp knife, trim off the excess pastry, then gently crimp all around the edge. Make a few small holes in the centre of the pie. Glaze the top with beaten egg.

7. Sprinkle the pie with sugar and bake in the centre of the oven for 45 minutes to 1 hour until golden brown all over and the apples are tender.

8. Serve with a generous helping of vanilla ice cream, custard or clotted cream.

DARCELLE

We met Darcelle's daughter Kiki in a hotel we were staying at in Nashville. She worked there and we got chatting. Soon enough, we were video calling Darcelle to beg and plead she take us in for an afternoon of pie making. She quite graciously agreed.

We had no idea we'd be crashing a birthday party when we invited ourselves over. Darcelle's great-grandbaby was celebrating her third birthday on the day we'd cornered her into sharing her special recipe with us. So into Candyland we went, a kitchen completely covered in giant papier-mâché sweeties and dotted with pastel-coloured balloons.

Grandkids and great-grandkids emerged from various rooms of the apartment as we rolled up our sleeves and rolled lemons underfoot. Still, the chaos didn't seem to bother Darcelle one bit. She whipped this icebox (fridge) pie up for us in barely no time at all between breaking up fights, placating crying babies and reassuring hormonal teens. All in a day's work for this granny.

Born: *Nashville, Tennessee, USA, 1957*
Mother tongue: *American English*
Grandchildren: *Joelniqua, Donta, Donquarius, Kyfaria, Kymiyah, Karea, Ariya, Jo'elle*
They call her: *Momma*

I learned to make this back when I was a teenager, from my mother. My momma would put this in an icebox when the summers would be long and hot here. That was before we could afford a refrigerator. It's no baking necessary and actually one of the easiest desserts to pull together. Especially when you have a big ol' family like ours and don't have so much time to be preparing desserts as well as lunches and dinners.

I love to get in the kitchen and cook but my arthritis makes it hard these days. Growing up, my kids had home-cooked meals every single day. I used to make homemade pizzas on Fridays. That would be the treat. Homemade back in those days was different to what it is today. My daughter's homemade is buying a box pizza from the store and adding a little topping to it. I would make my own dough,

roll it out – what it really means to homemake something. *Spaghetti tetrazzini* was my specialty and my sons still make that for their kids. That was spaghetti, shredded chicken and cream of mushroom soup. All baked together in the oven. My grandkids are not cooking at all. They're eating out. It's McDonald's and whatever else they get fast. It's a different situation now because everything has gotten so convenient.

I had babies around the same time I learned to make this pie. It was real early to be having babies. I was 16 years old when I had my first. I was a baby myself. I have so many great-grandbabies already and I think I have a good 20 years left in me, minimum. My grandmother lived until 102 and my mother is 87. I may well get to see another generation in my lifetime. Great-great-grandbabies. We celebrate children in this family but we're trying to break the cycle of having them so young. My daughter was 16 when she got pregnant, too.

When you have a lot of support, it's not so bad. The rule is to not continue to have them. It's worse having the babies later in your 30s because your nerves get pretty bad then. It makes a difference being young and having the energy and right mental attitude. When I fell pregnant so young, my family was supportive of me. My mother and father probably talked, but not where I could hear it. It's not about making a kid feel bad or feel worse than what they already feeling anyways. It's about the support that you give. With mine,

I've always been there for them. Anything I can do for them, I will still do today.

When the same thing happened to my daughter, I already knew before she figured out a way to tell me. I had been pregnant four times. I knew what it felt like and looked like. I could see it on her. I was just waiting on her to come clean and tell me. Still, I would rather them learn for themselves than me tell them everything that's going on out there in the world. It's the same for my grandkids, too.

Experience is the best thing and you get that all on your own. Having my kids and grandkids and great grandkids has been amazing.

To be able to be here to see them all grow is just the best experience I have ever had. A lot of kids don't get to even know their grand-mommas. I have this whole bunch of kids that I'm able to be a part of raising.

Men have come and go. You can't make somebody want you when they don't. Number one, I don't have time for foolishness and if that's going to take my mind elsewhere - no. You need to focus on your family. The minute you have kids, the focus goes away from men and onto those babies.
—

Momma Darcelle

MOMMA DARCELLE'S SOUTHERN LEMON ICEBOX PIE

INGREDIENTS
(Feeds 8-10)

— 70g (5 tbsp) butter, plus extra for greasing
— 300g (10oz) Hobnobs or digestives (Darcelle uses graham crackers, if you can find them)
— 2 tsp cinnamon
— 1 tsp salt

FOR THE FILLING

— 4 lemons (zest of 2 and juice of all 4)
— 2 x 397g (14oz) tins condensed milk

METHOD

1. Grease a 25cm (10in) loose-bottomed tart tin with a little butter. Melt the rest of the butter gently in a pan and set aside.

2. In a food processor, blitz the biscuits until ground but not powdery.

3. Tip into a mixing bowl and add the cinnamon and salt. Stir the butter in well.

4. Transfer to your prepared tart tin, pressing into the bottom and most of the way up the sides. Put in the fridge for 1 hour to set. Don't be confused by the 'icebox' title, this pie is set in the fridge.

5. Meanwhile, make the filling. Combine the lemon zest and juice in a mixing bowl. Add the condensed milk and stir well to combine. As you stir, the lemon will thicken the condensed milk.

6. When the biscuit case has firmed up, remove from the fridge and pour this mixture into it, distributing evenly with a spatula or the back of a spoon. Put the whole thing into the fridge for 2–3 hours until set.

7. Gently remove the icebox pie from the tin and put onto a plate (you could dust it with a little more cinnamon or grate over a little more lemon zest, if desired, to decorate). Slice the pie with a warm knife to make a clean cut and serve with squirty cream.

ANNE

New Orleans has this air of confidence about it. It knows it's fun, it's liberal, that it has history and traditions and defining flavours. In New Orleans, if you survived the hurricane and came back to the city, if you know how to dance with abandon at a street party and if you know the key ingredients that go into gumbo and jambalaya, you're all united.

Anne is an incarnation of her city. She was cool, calm and permanently on the verge of saying something cheeky. While her friend Harriet would recount a story, Anne was on hand to confirm facts and add the odd anecdote; hilarious asides added with the driest of deliveries. That Anne was head and shoulders taller than Harriet only added to their catching hilarity, particulalry when performing their flambé Bananas Foster routine.

Anne, who is also a tour guide for the city, was determined that by the time we left we would say 'New Orleans' properly. So, in case you don't know, it's not pronounced 'New Or-leans', it's 'New Orrrrrrrr-luns'.

Born: *New Orleans, Louisiana, USA, 1942*
Mother tongue: *American English*
Grandchildren: *Shelby, Barrett, Reese, Jack, Abby*
They call her: *Grandma*

Bananas Foster started in New Orleans because we're a port city. We were the banana port for the Caribbean - just 110 miles from the Gulf of Mexico. Quite big ships would come down the river and they'd get stuck for one reason or another and couldn't get to port. Which would be bad news for their bananas. Nobody wanted to buy overripe bananas - it was a serious issue. Thankfully, there was a man named Richard Foster who was good friends with a man called Owen Brennan who owned quite a famous New Orleans restaurant called Brennan's. He must have gotten a shipment of overripe bananas, so he told his friend Brennan to challenge the chef to come up with a recipe that meant they wouldn't go to waste.

Bananas Foster is now the dessert of the city. There's nothing to it. Any idiot can make it. One thing you must remember is you

absolutely cannot use green bananas. Also - don't forget the voodoo powder (the cinnamon). We have a history of voodoo here. When you walk down the street, if someone does this little hand shake at you, they're putting the juju on you. It's not a good sign.

New Orleans is just a different city. We're harmonious here and we have a *joie de vivre*. After Hurricane Katrina we were devastated but we celebrated Mardi Gras with parades and did everything as we would have, had the hurricane not hit. We lost 80 per cent of neighbour-hoods, but we still did it. We had to do it. It's our tradition. If we hadn't celebrated Mardi Gras, it would have been doom and gloom, but we all came together for this.

In fact, it's just as much a part of our history as it is our food – this notion of 'coming together'. Creole is a way of distinguishing those born here in the New Territory from the 1700s onwards. You were Creole whether you were English, French, Spanish or West African or mixed. I'm Cajun, German and Irish. I'm a gumbo of cultures and this is typical of Louisiana. The original Cajuns were French peasants that left Normandy and Brittany in France in the early 1600s. They moved to what is today Nova Scotia, Canada. They meant to settle up there, and lived there totally undisturbed for around 100 years, until the English gained that territory. They moved south to the French Colonies in Louisiana because we were French-speaking.

They settled in prairies and swamps. They remained isolated and nobody bothered with them, so much so that the majority didn't even speak English. My grandmother didn't speak English at all. In fact, people still speak French in Cajun country.

I'm just like my daddy - the Irish and Cajun come out. My mum died two years before Daddy. At the time, someone came up to my daddy. She said, 'How's Irene?' He responded, 'Dead.' We just tell it how it is. We celebrate life here in New Orleans - and death is just as much a part of it.

The death of my grandchild was the hardest thing I've lived through, though. She had lymphoma. She died at the age of 15 of a brain haemorrhage. It was traumatic. I was so worried about my daughter-in-law, who went through such a depression that she was almost hospitalised. My family is almost the exact opposite. We just blurt what we feel out and don't keep any of it in. What can we do about it but go on? She's dead. In my family, if you're dead, you're dead. I think younger generations now think and analyse things too much. I just went through life. That's just how I did it. You keep going.

—

Grandma Anne

GRANDMA ANNE'S CARAMELISED
BANANA FLAMBÉ (*Bananas Foster*)

INGREDIENTS
(*Feeds 4*)

— 100g (7 tbsp) butter
— 200g (1 cup) brown sugar
— 2 ripe bananas, sliced into
  1cm (½in) rounds
— ½ tsp vanilla essence
— pinch sea salt
— 120ml (½ cup) banana liqueur
— 200ml (¾ cup + 2 tbsp) rum
— pinch cinnamon

METHOD

1. Melt the butter in a large frying pan on medium heat and add the sugar to form a paste. Let the mixture thicken a little and caramelise for about 3 minutes.

2. Working quickly, turn up the heat and fold in the banana slices, vanilla essence and a pinch of sea salt – don't cook those bananas too long.

3. Gather your audience and be ready with a match or lighter. Turn the heat off if you have a gas hob and pour the liqueur and rum into the middle of the pan. Turn the heat back on high. Ignite to flambé! It should take easily.

4. Simply shake to keep the flame burning and to evenly distribute the liquid round the pan. Watch the sparkle that happens as you (carefully) throw a generous pinch of cinnamon into the flame.

5. Once the flame has gone out it means the alcohol has burned off and you are ready to serve. Divide between dishes with a scoop of vanilla ice cream on top, followed by a drizzle of the sauce.

Tip: You can also make this with thin slices of apple instead of banana.

Bibi Ayda's Iraqi Orange and Walnut Bundt Cake

Safia Shakarchi, baker, food writer and photographer

Ingredients

- 250g (1 cup + 2 tbsp) very soft butter
- 340g (1¾ cups) caster sugar
- zest of 2 oranges
- 5 eggs
- 340g (2⅓ cups) flour
- 2 tsp baking powder
- a handful of walnuts, roughly chopped (approximately 75g/⅔ cup)

For all her grace and charm and elegance, Bibi was a mess in the kitchen. I'm not entirely sure I've inherited the former qualities, but I've undoubtedly inherited the latter. Spice jars open on the counter, a bag of fava beans half podded on the kitchen table, cupboards left slightly ajar and a fridge a little too full. Bibi's excess was testament to her all-consuming love for feeding, for food and for us, her grandchildren. She was chaos and yet perfectly put together all at once, and her cooking just the same. Her *kleicha* (classic Iraqi biscuits) were always ever so slightly wonky and her *biryani* piled high and spilling over the edges of the platter, but to this day I've never had food as incredible as hers.

Bibi's life was not easy, and although I never got to ask her, I sense that she found peace in the kitchen. She might have made a mess, but cooking was precisely how she made sense of the troubles she endured, and I will always be grateful that she passed that affinity for food onto me.

My mum and aunt can recite the recipe for this orange cake word for word, measured in packs, spoonfuls and handfuls. It would often be waiting for us after the feast Bibi had cooked up for dinner, and it came out perfectly imperfect every time.

You'll need a Bundt tin to make this.

Feeds 8-10

1. Preheat oven to 180°C/160°C fan/350°F/gas 4.

2. Use some of the softened butter to grease the inside of a Bundt tin very well, making sure to get into all the creases.

3. Beat the remaining butter together with the sugar until pale and fluffy either by hand, using an electric whisk, or in the bowl of a stand mixer. Scrape down the sides, grate in the orange zest and mix once more.

4. Add in the eggs 1 at a time, beating after each addition and scraping down the sides regularly. Don't worry if the mixture begins to curdle.

5. In a separate bowl, briefly mix together the flour and baking powder to ensure the ingredients are evenly incorporated. Fold the dry ingredients into the wet ingredients in 3 stages, being careful not to over-mix. Finally, gently fold through the walnut pieces.

6. Pour the batter into the prepared Bundt tin and spread into an even layer with a spatula or spoon. Bake in the preheated oven for 40–50 minutes, or until a skewer inserted into the middle of the cake comes out clean.

7. Leave to cool in the tin for 10–15 minutes before turning out onto a wire rack to cool completely. Enjoy with a lovely cup of tea.

NICOLETTA

As we learned to prepare Nicoletta's favourite Sicilian dessert, she was also intermittently checking on her husband setting the table ('He always does this - he didn't wait for the dishwasher to finish before taking out the cutlery'), making dinner for the evening and texting the boiler man to come and fix a problem with the heating.

It would have been the ultimate scene of everyday domesticity, were it not played out for us in a 16th-century Sicilian palace by the Italian Duchess of Palma. 'Unfortunately, modern duchesses don't have time to polish their nails,' she shrugged while shoving a tray of rosemary-seasoned potatoes in the oven, brewing us a tea and ordering her husband to, 'just please wait for the dishwasher to finish its cycle.'

This cooking duchess invited us into her palace for a special culinary masterclass spiced with Sicilian history, calling each of us 'piccolina' and driving home just how important it is to cook when you're a 'mamma'. Her spirit is every bit that of a true matriarch and her fierce energy is enough to dispel any image of a puffed-up aristocrat lethargically lounging on a chaise longue. In short, we absolutely love her.

Born: *Venice, Italy, 1952*
Mother tongue: *Italian*
Grandchildren: *Isabella, Gioacchino*
They call her: *Nonna Nico*

Both my grandmothers were excellent cooks. One was better at French-style cooking and the other was from Tuscany. My maternal grandmother passed away when I was nine, but I picked up the Tuscan recipes as they were passed down in the family. I do always regret not asking for the recipes of my paternal grandmother because she had such a refined way of preparing food. My own step-grandchildren love my *gelo di mellone*, which is a Sicilian dessert. I'm Venetian, but since I've been living here in Sicily for so many years, I've learned to cook local dishes. It's a delicious watermelon pudding infused with jasmine.

Sometimes people are surprised to hear that I'm a duchess, but I tell them that modern duchesses don't have time to sit around painting their nails. My husband Duke Gioacchino Tomasi di Lampedusa has inherited the 18th-century palazzo of his adopted father and Italy's most famed writer, Giuseppe Tomasi di Lampedusa - author of *Il Gattopardo* (*The Leopard*). We must do all we can to maintain it and to keep his memory alive. The cooking workshops I run here are a part of that.

I've always loved food as a very important cultural aspect of a country. Through food and the cuisine of a country you understand its history and its culture. It's exactly what I want to do in my cooking classes. My lessons are focusing on Sicilian culture and history through food. We make traditional dishes, like Palermitan street-food favourite *panelle*, or a selection of pastas inspired by different regions of Sicily. I also really believe in cooking local and using ingredients that make sense to the season.

I myself have a huge collection of cookbooks. I love them as books. I like the ones that also tell stories and ones that reflect my way of understanding a cuisine. I enjoy learning about the history of a dish. For example, this *gelo di mellone* I am cooking for you today would not exist were it not for the Arabs that came to Sicily over 1,000 years ago. Sicilian cuisine has been heavily influenced by the Arabs, who brought practically half of the ingredients that are now staples of the Sicilian kitchen. Jasmine, which features heavily in this dish, was introduced by the Arabs. Other staples like almonds and pistachios also came here with the Arabs.

It has been said by my son that I'm the only mamma that's ready to cook at any time of the night or morning. I love to host very much. I always love to cook and love when my son brings his friends. I've cooked a whole meal for him and his friends at three in the morning. He was one of the most popular kids in the American school because he would trade my beautiful food for all this horrible junk food, like peanut butter-jelly sandwiches. At a certain point, one of the other mothers stopped me and asked me for my meatball recipes. I said, 'How do you know about my meatballs?' to which she responded that all the children were eating my food. Of course he'd give the blonde girls with blue eyes two meatballs. Food is love, after all.

Feeding is an expression of love. It's an Italian thing. Here, it's important to feed. Did you know, for example, that one of the first symptoms of mental disorder is a bad relationship with food? How you approach food in life can say a lot about your mental state and your personality. Then of course, there is the inescapable fact that we can't live without food.
—

Nonna Nico

NONNA NICO'S SICILIAN JASMINE-INFUSED
WATERMELON JELLY (*Gelo di mellone*)

INGREDIENTS
(*Feeds 6*)

- 1 2½-3kg (5½-6½lb) watermelon, flesh deseeded and roughly chopped
- 1 handful jasmine flowers, plus some for decoration (optional)
- 150-200g (¾-1 cup) granulated sugar, depending on the sweetness of the watermelon
- 75g (heaped ½ cup) cornflour
- 100g (3½oz) dark chocolate chips, or shards of finely chopped dark chocolate

METHOD

1. Push your chopped watermelon flesh through a fine-mesh sieve or whizz in a blender until smooth and measure out 1l (4 cups) of juice. If you have extra, save it, chill it and serve with mint for a refreshing drink.

2. Put the juice in a large bowl with the jasmine flowers and let steep for a few hours, then remove and discard the flowers.

3. Pour the juice into a saucepan, add the sugar to taste and whisk in the cornflour. Cook over a low heat, stirring constantly until it comes to a boil and thickens. Time 1 minute and remove from the heat.

4. Pour into a large glass bowl or individual ramekins (or champagne saucers for glamorous presentation!) and let cool. Refrigerate until set and cold.

5. Before serving, garnish with chocolate chips (to imitate the watermelon seeds) and jasmine flowers.

Granny Charlotte's Chocolate and Chestnut Mousse Cake

Merlin Labron-Johnson, chef

Ingredients

— 250g (2 cups) chestnuts, cooked and peeled
— 250ml (1 cup + 1 tbsp) milk
— 250g (1 cup + 1 tbsp) unsalted butter, diced
— 250g (9oz) dark chocolate, chopped
— 4 eggs, separated
— 140g (¾ cup) caster sugar
— 300g (1¼ cups) thick crème fraîche
— 50ml (3 tbsp) dark rum
— chocolate for shaving

This recipe is adapted from something my grandmother made for my 28th birthday. She lives in the French Pyrenees and had collected fallen chestnuts that morning while walking the dog in the forest. It was of a magic, mousse-like texture that disappeared from your mouth as you ate it, leaving behind only the delicate flavour of chestnuts, forest floor and rum.

Granny didn't use a recipe for this cake, she just knew what to do. I suppose that's what 70 years of cooking experience does for you. With a little persuasion, she wrote down what she had made and added it to her tatty old recipe file. She doesn't use cookbooks, but she will often consult this file, which is splattered with sauce and filled with cut-outs from magazines, rough methods and ideas scribbled down over decades.

I adapted her chestnut cake recipe by adding chocolate, because I love chocolate. If it is not chestnut season you can use cooked vacuum-packed or canned chestnuts, which are readily available in supermarkets and much easier to work with. For this recipe you'll need a springform cake tin, lined on the bottom with greaseproof paper.

Feeds 8—10

1. Preheat oven to 160°C/140°C fan/325°F/gas 3.

2. Put the chestnuts in a saucepan with the milk and bring to a simmer. Cook gently for 10 minutes and place in a blender. Blend until smooth, adding a little extra milk if necessary, and set aside.

3. Put the butter and chocolate in a heatproof bowl and place over simmering water, stirring from time to time until it is melted.

4. In a large bowl, whisk the egg yolks with the caster sugar and then incorporate the chestnut purée, followed by the chocolate–butter mixture. Whisk the egg whites to soft peaks and, using a spatula, gently fold it into the chocolate and chestnut batter. Pour the mixture into the cake tin and place it in the oven for 30 minutes. To check if it's cooked enough, insert a skewer or the tip of a small knife. If it comes out clean, it is ready; if not, return to the oven for a few minutes more. Leave to cool for 45 minutes to 1 hour.

5. Mix the crème fraîche with the rum and spread over the top of the cake. Decorate with chocolate shavings. This cake is best eaten on the day it is made, which, if past experience is anything to go by, shouldn't be a problem.

JENNY

Jenny gave us some pretty wild instructions down the phone on how to arrive at her house in a quiet British village a few hours out of London. We had assured her we only needed a postcode to pinpoint her with the sat nav, but she insisted on reeling off the directions she had memorised all of her life, down to which coloured gate to turn at and which tree to stop at following turning right at the school.

On a typically soggy day for southern England, we were welcomed into the warmth of Jenny's kitchen, thoroughly toasty thanks to an old Aga that is never switched off. She was fresh from her daily three-hour ramble with Toby the terrier, so dripping wet in an anorak, she let us in, past the chainsaws and the jam cupboard, for a cup of tea and an afternoon of meringue making.

Hardened in her country manner but soft and maternal in her sentiment, Jenny let us in on so many secrets this day. In spite of being a seasoned chainsaw wielder, she's also a committed mother and grandmother. She laid on an enormous spread for us and admitted her relationship with her own mother had been so fraught that it had taught her to be a better mother to her own children. She had never had dessert as a child, so in her adult life, in role of mummy and granny, she became the Queen of Puddings, whizz with a whisk and master of all things sweet.

Born: *Leeds, UK, 1941*
Mother tongue: *English*
Grandchildren: *Millie, Oscar, Cecilie, Ottilie*
They call her: *Granny Jen Jen*

I don't have much of a sweet tooth, but as soon as I started cooking, pudding came instinctively. I never ate dessert growing up, so I wanted that for my children. There has always been one with every meal ever since. That's why they call me the Queen of Puddings. I make my own jam for this queen of puddings and if you look in one of my cupboards, it's full of my homemade jam.

I've never bought processed foods – not even biscuits. I make it all myself. I haven't bought a loaf of bread in 40 years, or a jar of jam. I think it's important for a mum to know how to do all of these things. I used to have a pig in the back garden and

would have it slaughtered in the yard. I've always liked the rural life. They call me 'Chainsaw Jenny' because I have three chainsaws and I'm not afraid to use them.

I was neurotic about my children's teeth and their health in general. I wanted them to have beautiful teeth and be fed well. I think you show your love with nutritious meals. Not just tasty meals, but homemade meals. People now are so obese. Don't they have mirrors in their homes?

I've always been maternal and I tried hard to be a different mother to my children because I didn't have a good childhood or a great

relationship with my own mother. She never bonded with me, so I made a special effort to bond with mine. I never went to work. My mother worked into her 70s. I don't regret not having a good relationship with my mother. It was never meant to be. She just wasn't maternal. I felt like she never really wanted me.

I remember the very first time my dad held my hand I was 13 and we were crossing the road in Nottingham. Once we got to the pavement he dropped my hand and he never held it again. It was the only time I'd ever held his hand. When I saw him before he died all I wanted to do was tell him how much I loved him, but I couldn't. I was too emotionally stilted. I'll always regret it, but it's the way I was raised. As my mother said, 'We're not a kissy family.'

I left home as soon as I could. My husband, Iver Wilde, was older than me by 15 years. I worked on his farm as a dairymaid and he was married. It was very rare back then, but we had an affair. He made the first move and kissed me, which was very unexpected because I was in the cowshed milking the cows at the time. He was the first and only man I have ever been with and he was married to someone else. We couldn't well meet in his house, so until we married, it was the hay shed. Wilde by name, wild by nature.

He had three children by a previous marriage and I consider them all my own. He was very loving and intelligent and he came from such a loving family. They never rowed. My parents rowed every day and so my brother and I ended up completely neurotic. He really was the perfect match for me in that sense.

—

Granny Jen Jen

GRANNY JEN JEN'S
ENGLISH QUEEN OF PUDDINGS

INGREDIENTS
(Feeds 6)

— 25g (2 tbsp) unsalted butter,
  plus extra for greasing
— 600ml (2½ cups) whole milk
— zest of 2 lemons
— 90g (scant ½ cup) caster
  sugar, plus extra for dusting
— 150g (1¼ cups) homemade
  white breadcrumbs (great for
  using up stale bread)
— 3 eggs, separated
— 6 tbsp raspberry jam (Jenny's
  was homemade, of course)

METHOD

1. Grease a 22cm (9in) pie dish with a little butter and preheat oven to 180°C/
   160°C fan/350°F/gas 4.

2. Warm the milk in a medium saucepan, then add the butter, lemon zest
   and half of the caster sugar. Stir until the sugar has dissolved.

3. Now mix in the breadcrumbs and turn off the heat. Leave for 15–20 minutes
   to soak and cool a little.

4. When the time is up, whisk the egg yolks in a small bowl and stir them into
   the cooled mixture. Then pour everything into the buttered pie dish and put
   in the oven for 30 minutes to cook until set.

5. Remove from the oven and put to one side while you whip up the meringue.
   Using an electric whisk, beat the egg whites in a clean bowl until stiff enough
   to hold over your head. Whisk in the remaining half of the caster sugar.

6. Take your pie dish and spread a layer of raspberry jam over the custardy
   base. Then spoon the meringue mixture on top of this, spreading it from
   the middle outwards.

7. Sprinkle with 1 tsp caster sugar and bake for 15 minutes, or until golden brown
   and slightly crisp on top.

8. Serve warm from the oven with cream, ice cream or custard.

Abuela Tatá's Uruguayan Peach Ice Cream

Francis Mallmann, chef

Ingredients

— 8 ripe peaches, stoned:
   6 for the ice cream,
   2 for serving
— 1l (4 cups) double cream
— knob butter
— fresh mint for garnish

The recipe needs no knife, only your hands, a fork and a whisk. You can use any freezer container or a loaf tin lined with greaseproof paper.

There is a country in South America that is called Uruguay, where my grandma was born. Not only that, but it has some of the most delicious peaches to be mouthed. The best variety is called Rey del Monte and they come from Bella Unión (Artigas) and are available only during the last two weeks of January. The truly luscious ones come from dry summers with lots of sunshine, when taste concentrates so scrumptiously that they make you silently faint with pleasure as the juices drip from hands, lips and heart.

My grandma – Tatá or Chucha, as we called her – was one of the hurried types. She walked fast around her house in the old city of Montevideo, as she sewed, cleaned or read, talking to herself, doing as many things as she could on the long, hot summer days.

Only when these peaches were at their best, she would peel six of them with her fingers, roughly mash their tender flesh with a fork, and add them to 35 ounces of the best Conaprole double cream, cold and beaten with a wire whisk until it was stiff. The mix would go into the rectangular tins used for ice cubes and into the humble freezer of her fridge that – white when new – had turned into an ancient, suspicious yellow, with a big metal-handled door that made a great click when closing it. She would serve it with a very light syrup that had been slightly burned, giving it the most interesting and romantic taste.

Nowadays, after so many years of cooking with fires, I like to serve the ice cream with some extra-fresh peaches that I open in half with my fingers and burn very fast on a griddle with sugar and butter. The technique requires them to be glazed only on the open side, so they remain raw and slightly warm. When I lay them by the scoop of ice cream on the plate, they look like the most passionate, elegant, glazy, moist brides in slight summer dresses, with an array of green from the fresh hand-ripped mint. Yes, I fall in love every day.

I can only thank life for having nested me as a child in this beautiful, tiny country with such a loving grandma who taught me taste and left me, as inheritance, a reverie of ripe peaches that no other child has ever had.

Feeds 8-10

1. Mash 6 of the peaches with a fork.

2. Whisk the double cream until stiff.

3. Fold the peaches into the cream and put into a metal ice-cream tray or tin in the freezer.

4. When ready to serve, heat a knob of butter in a griddle pan. Break 2 peaches in half, discard the stones, sprinkle the flesh with brown sugar and place flesh-side down in the pan to caramelise for a couple of minutes.

5. Serve next to the ice cream with ripped mint.

MUALLA

The very last in our gaggle of grannies but certainly not least, Mualla in Istanbul book-ended our three years around the world, cooking with grandmothers. It makes sense then, after a book rich in recipes and wisdom, that we end on her ultra-light semolina *helva*.

The day we cooked with Mualla it poured but that mattered very little. Having been welcomed into such a warm home packed with women all eager to share the culinary delights of Istanbul, we revelled in the now well-known high that comes with the sharing of special recipes across generations. We downed sweet tea looking over the Bosphorus. We danced to 'Hey Mambo, Mambo Italiano', Mualla - despite being unsteady on her feet at the ripe age of 92 - leading the charge.

Our days with Mualla and her granddaughter Zeynep will have a lasting impression. Their readiness to fling their doors and arms wide open to us, show us around their city and introduce us to friends, family and favourite foods is one that has been echoed throughout the process of making this book.

The immense hospitality, kindness and openness of those we cook with never cease to surprise us. It has been an affirmation that there is value in what we are doing, that these dishes are more than a quick feed. They are the very embodiment of a full life. They are loaded with memories, feeling and the most precious things that life affords us: time and love.

Born: *Istanbul, Turkey, 1928*
Mother tongue: *Turkish*
Grandchildren: *Seyfi, Zeynep*
They call her: *Anneanne*

Everybody here makes *helva* but my grandchildren say no one does it like me. They always get upset that I might not be telling them something top-secret in the recipe because they say theirs never tastes as good as my own. In Turkey we make it for religious holidays like Kandil or for funerals but I make it for the grandchildren every week.

Most people use milk instead of water for *helva*, but with milk it tastes a little more like pudding, it's more creamy. This version is from the Black Sea region, which is where my mother was from, and this is her recipe. She was a master in the kitchen. She was always the host and I learned to make special sweet dishes from her.

My mother was such a strong woman that she became our friend, sister and father all in one because my father died when we were just girls. She had her first child at the age of 13 so there really weren't many years between us and our own mother. She could relate to us and we loved her for that. I didn't go to college so that my mum wouldn't go mad at home on her own. She begged that we wouldn't all go off and so I didn't.

Back then, we lived a fairy-tale existence. Istanbul was all green. Now it's a concrete jungle that is unsafe. There are so many high-rise buildings, it adds to how threatening the city has become. As teenagers, we would be out having fun but now we're worried about women going out in the evenings in case they become the target of an attack.

I lived the first years of Atatürk's Turkish republic. Equal rights for women were introduced into Turkey in my childhood. In Ottoman times, women would wear these very colourful shawls to cover their heads. Within a couple of months of Atatürk coming in, our style suddenly became European. We could wear skirts. We could show off our hair-dos. I remember my father bought my mother a shoulderless gown to wear when the new laws came into place. It was a time of freedom and hope and frivolity.

Now we're going back to the olden days. More women walk around like cockroaches, covered up and scuttling in fear of men. I pray five times a day and I am Muslim but my religion doesn't involve me doing this. They want us to turn into Arabs here in Turkey. They never wanted this as a modern nation and so once Atatürk died, everything started to slowly and discreetly unravel and rewind. People have become more conservative. They're now actually debating in the government if men can marry six-year-old girls. Imagine, the Turkey we live in now.

The most important lesson I've learned in life is to be a good person. My mother taught me to treat everyone as equal and never look down on anyone. Be humble. It's the best thing you can be. If the people surrounding me are happy and well, I am happy because that's all I need. This might be why I have made so many friends in life. At the hospital where I go for dialysis every week, I make friends with all the doctors and nurses. They all now have my number and call me for advice. It's like I have all of these adopted grandchildren as well as my own.
—

Anneanne Mualla

ANNEANNE MUALLA'S TURKISH SEMOLINA PUDDING (*Helva*)

INGREDIENTS
(Feeds 8-10)

— 450g (2¼ cups) sugar, caster
  or granulated
— 250g (1 cup + 2 tbsp) unsalted
  butter, kept as a block
— 650ml (2¾ cups) water
— 500g (2¾ cups) semolina,
  coarse or fine
— 25g (¼ cup) pine nuts

METHOD

1. In a medium pan, put the sugar, butter and water over medium heat. Bring to the boil slowly to melt the butter and dissolve the sugar. When it turns bubbly and smells milky, turn off the heat.

2. Meanwhile, take a non-stick pan with a lid and tip in the semolina and pine nuts. You're going to dry-roast the semolina on a medium heat, stirring at all times so it doesn't burn. You'll know when it's ready because you'll smell it toasting, and it will start to go golden and the pine nuts will take on a slight pinkish hue. This will take about 30 minutes (yes, that long).

3. When the semolina is nearly ready, reheat the butter mixture, then pour it slowly into the semolina pan (Mualla asked her granddaughter to pour while she stirred). Stir well to make sure it's combined, then let it bubble and settle before turning the heat off. Put the lid on and leave to stand for 10–15 minutes, until the liquid is absorbed. Every 5 minutes or so, stir to check it hasn't got too solid, breaking up the mixture. It should be dry enough for you to fluff up nicely with a spoon or fork.

4. Serve warm in bowls with a sprinkle of cinnamon – and a scoop of vanilla ice cream if you like.

MY GRANDMOTHERS' RECIPES

MY GRANDMOTHERS' RECIPES

THANK YOU

Thanks to all the grandmothers who opened their homes, kitchens and hearts to us. We are years wiser because of the time you gave to us.

Thank you to our photographers. To our great pal Ella Sullivan and her Mamiya. Receiving those first film scans made us even more certain that this was a project we had to do. It is always funny seeing a granny's face when Ella takes her shoes off to stand on the table to get the shot from above. To Nina Raasch - calm, considered, all in black - who photographed Ania in Poland and Ester and Edna in Tel Aviv. To Issy Croker for being very up for shooting Jenny in the greenhouse mid-British downpour. To Maureen Evans for being on hand in Mexico City to capture Betsy with such beauty. To videographer Nathan, for putting our film together with such ease.

Thank you to the lovely Jasmine Philips for methodical recipe testing, making sense out of some rather manically scribbled recipes. Such a pleasure to work with.

Thanks to Ben and David for your patience and creative direction in the never-ending iterations of our crowdfunding film and for those first pledges.

Love to our other grandmothers.

To Anastasia's great Granny Doris, the Harrison family anchor who was old as far back as Anastasia can remember, with a permanent supply of ginger biscuits and lemonade for all grandchildren visiting. In spite of being tiny, frail and housebound, she loved her food right the way up until the ripe old age of 99. Fish and chips were devoured with her in the company of Tina the cat. And to Granny Joan, who has never been the best of cooks but knew her way round a good jacket potato.

To Iska's paternal granny, Lally Settle (Helen), mother of four boys, purveyor of soup, very short, insanely practical, completely selfless, still knitting, watercolour painting and doing crosswords aged 97. And to wondrous Great-Aunt Rosamund, who had neat Glen's vodka on ice with mackerel pâté and Mini Cheddars every day at 6 p.m. She introduced Iska to lapsang souchong tea, fur coats and chicken fricassée, and once served cauliflower from a skip.

GRAN
KNOWLEDGE
MENTS

In memory of Doris Harrison. Happy childhood days spent baking butterfly buns, jam tarts, apple pies, chocolate cake and mince pies at Christmas. Love you and miss you so much, Gran.

—

Beverley x

Bell White

—

David Butler

To my Antigoni & Sophia you are my inspiration & my heart x

—

Tonia Buxton

Stella Gattegno

—

Daniela Gattegno

Granny Pam and Nanna Rita – for their strawberry shortbread and their taste in tabards.

—

Ben Kendall

To my gran (Doris Harrison), for rolling up our sleeves, putting on our pinnies, standing us on stools when we were far too small to reach the kitchen worktop and taking the time to cake bake with us – jam tarts, fairy cakes and, on special occasions, her delicious chocolate cake.
I do so miss these cake-baking days with you, Gran.

—

Barbara Miaris

Mualla Şenyiğit

—

Zeynep Moroglu

Felicity Crawley

—

Jessica Phillips

DEDICATIONS

Pavilion

Our local East London bakery that supported us back when Anastasia was baking endless loaves of sourdough. Your cardamom buns fuelled the very first brainstorms for this book.

—

wearethepavilion.com

Isle of Olive

Our home away from home, the Isle of Olive deli offers the closest thing to Yiayia's Greek kitchen when we're in London. Thank you for the spanakopita and baklava experience on Broadway Market, and for supporting this book.

—

isleofolive.co.uk

Alambique

A supporter of *Grand Dishes* from almost the very beginning, Alambique is the culinary school and shop in the heart of Madrid founded by Abuela Clara María González de Amezúa. Many thanks to daughter Maria for arranging our unforgettable weekend.

—

alambique.com

CPC Cooking Ideas

Thank you to Food & Wine PR experts CPC Cooking Ideas for the introduction to their lovely brand ambassador, Abuela Clara María González de Amezúa, and a fine weekend in Madrid.

—

cpccookingideas.com

Allegra Pomilio - Mèlisses Andros

A fellow Grecophile who saw something special in *Grand Dishes* and shares the same values of hospitality and love of foraging and home cooking that we do. An adopted Greek, who really understands the concept of 'Filoxenia'.

—

melissesandros.com

Brand USA

For pulling together an itinerary that we could barely keep up with and for expanding our waistbands to epic proportions on our Great Granny Road Trip. We could not have discovered America and its grannies without you.

—

visittheUSA.co.uk

Hertz

Our Ford Fiesta just about pulled us and our many suitcases through five weeks of travel across America's Bible Belt. Thank you for our Black Beauty - we loved her and her slight frame in comparison to the monster trucks taking up the highway beside us.

—

hertz.com

The Outer Banks

Without your help, we would never have had the pleasure of deep diving into the culture, history and traditions of the American south with dear Sharon. We could not have wished for a more perfect welcome to the USA than this thoughtful and philosophical lady who knows her way around a shrimp or two.

—

outerbanks.org

Visit Houston
Thanks for showing us the true meaning of Tex Mex and introducing us to two of the sassiest grannies we have met writing this book. We won't remember Houston for NASA; it will be Irma's margarita and guacamole that will be forever etched in our memory.

—

visithoustontexas.com
irmasoriginal.com

Travel Texas
Thanks for finding the powerhouse that is Tootsie, for the most delectable barbecue we will ever have the pleasure of experiencing (at Snow's BBQ in Lexington) and for the stay of our lives at Dos Brisas. We experienced the best of Texas thanks to your expert advice and insights.

—

traveltexas.com

Rocca delle Tre Contrade
To the most tasteful villa in Sicily, thank you for your support and for sparing Dora to teach us the secret to silken *caponata*.

—

trecontrade.com

Go Israel
Many thanks for hooking us up with Edna, her peppers and a family that was so welcoming, it was enough to warm us on Tel Aviv's windiest day.

—

goisrael.com

Fujifilm
The images Ella and Nina captured on their vintage Mamiya cameras are thanks to you, for really, truly believing in the power of film. Much like our grannies, film photography is alive and full of feeling. Thank you for the many, many rolls.

—

fujifilm.eu/uk

Cointreau Family
We will never forget the weekend we spent with your family, from our first-ever first-class train journey to Paris, to being immersed in the glowing, orange hue of the Cointreau Crew. Thank you to Alfred for opening up your home, your garage and your bar to us. And to Gwen for translation and lessons in elegance and class.

—

cointreau.com

Polka Pants
To Maxine, who gifted us the comfiest, most stylish pants to cook in and got our grannies on the chef pant action too. We are so happy to be a part of your tribe of brilliant women working in food.

—

polkapants.com

The Ginger Pig
June insisted she wanted 'only the best' meat for her pie, and so as her favourite local butcher, you stepped up to the plate. Thanks for all that you did in the very earliest stages of *Grand Dishes* to support the project and for that delicious bit of beef.

—

thegingerpig.co.uk

New Orleans & Company
For raucous nights in New Orleans, for the music, the spontaneous poems about grandmothers performed for us in the streets and for hooking us up with a mighty gumbo (or two!). We love your city.

—

neworleans.com

The New Orleans School of Cooking
What a pleasure it was to be welcomed with open arms into the zany world of your sparring duo, Anne and Harriet. If we ever hear of anyone heading to NOLA, we shall be sending them to Anne and Harriet for a cooking class. We will never forget the juju.

—

neworleansschoolofcooking.com

Campaign to End Loneliness
Thank you for addressing a cause that is so close to our hearts: loneliness in old age. Here's to spending time in the good company of grannies everywhere.

—

campaigntoendloneliness.org

A NOTE ON THE AUTHORS

ANASTASIA MIARI

Based between Athens and London, journalist Anastasia Miari freelances for the *Independent*, the *Guardian*, the *Telegraph* and *Monocle* in the UK as well as *The New York Times* and the *National* further afield. Her travel- and food-focused stories – usually character-driven – also feature in Lonely Planet, *Suitcase* magazine and Soho House's *House Notes* magazine. Her first book, the *Wallpaper Guide to Athens*, was published by Phaidon in 2020 and her work spans beyond the written word to radio, podcasts and the occasional short film made with co-author Iska Lupton.

ISKA LUPTON

Iska Lupton is a creative director whose work focuses on food. From styling and writing to short films and events, she uses food as a medium for storytelling and entertainment. Iska runs a small agency designing multisensory experiences for brands such as Peroni Nastro Azzurro, Airbnb and Nike. In 2019 she trained as a cook with (grandmother) Darina Allen at Ballymaloe Cookery School in Ireland, before cooking at Sicilian villa Rocca delle Tre Contrade for a summer with Dora (on page 64).

Unbound is the world's first crowdfunding publisher, established in 2011.

We believe that wonderful things can happen when you clear a path for people who share a passion. That's why we've built a platform that brings together readers and authors to crowdfund books they believe in – and give fresh ideas that don't fit the traditional mould the chance they deserve.

This book is in your hands because readers made it possible. Everyone who pledged their support is listed below. Join them by visiting unbound.com and supporting a book today.